THE Mystery We Proclaim, SECOND EDITION

Catechesis for the Third Millennium

Francis D. Kelly

Our Sunday Visitor Publishing Division
Our Sunday Visitor, Inc.
Huntington, Indiana 46750

Nihil Obstat: Rev. George P. Evans, S.T.D.
Censor Librorum

Imprimatur: ✠ Bernard Cardinal Law
Archbishop of Boston
June 21, 1999

International Standard Book Number: 0-87973-597-X
Library of Congress Catalog Card Number: 99-74477

Cover and jacket design by Monica Watts; jacket illustration, "Icon of the Holy Trinity," by Eltchaninoff-Struve, reprinted by permission of St. Vladimir's Seminary Press, Crestwood, Tuckahoe, N.Y.

PRINTED IN THE UNITED STATES OF AMERICA

Table of Contents

Introduction

Within the past decade, two events have occurred which will have a lasting impact on catechesis for the foreseeable future: the promulgation of the *Catechism of the Catholic Church* and the issuance of the new *General Directory for Catechesis.*

In 1992, having had the privilege of serving as a consultant to the Redaction Committee of the *Catechism*, I published the first edition of *The Mystery We Proclaim.* It was intended to help catechists integrate the dominant themes and approach of the *Catechism* into their catechetical ministry. It apparently proved useful for catechist training courses and as background reading for those involved in this wonderful ministry in the Church.

I am happy to respond to the request of the publishers to produce a revised and expanded version of *The Mystery We Proclaim* based on our greater familiarity with and use of the *Catechism* and also on the new *General Directory for Catechesis.*

This book is no substitute for personal familiarity with and reading of the *Catechism* and the *Directory.* I hope, however, that it may be a useful companion for that reading, bringing together and highlighting some of the themes of both documents into a practical synthesis.

This book is also a personal and pastoral reflection on the part of the author, who has devoted twenty-five years of his priesthood to this central area of Church life. It does not pretend to be an exhaustive or detailed survey of the entire catechetical enterprise. It is to be hoped, however, that the very structure and ordering of these reflections and their dominant emphases will be a useful contribution to the ongoing discussion about the renewal of the catechetical apostolate.

In this book I have used a thoroughly ecclesial approach. My inspiration and references are often from the records of our Catholic tradition and from the writings of recent Popes. This reflects my belief that catechesis is above all a service in and for the Church by which she transmits her living faith from generation to generation.

I thank His Eminence Bernard Cardinal Law, who first introduced the concept of the *Catechism* at the Synod of 1985; Bishop Daniel Reilly of Worcester, my diocesan bishop; Father Alfred McBride, O.Praem., for his critical reading of the text; and Mrs. Maureen Terry for technical assistance.

Finally, I offer this ministerial effort to the patronage of the Blessed Virgin Mary, who first brought the Eternal Word to the human family and has no greater desire than to bring us to Him.

Monsignor Francis D. Kelly
Easter, 1999
Boston

Part One
Catechetics in a New Content

Chapter 1

The Impact of the *Catechism of the Catholic Church* and the *General Directory for Catechesis*

With the promulgation of the *Catechism of the Catholic Church* in 1992, and the new *General Directory for Catechesis* in 1997, the catechetical ministry functions in a wholly new context as we enter the Third Millennium.

Catechists now have in these two documents a clear vision and specific direction for their catechetical efforts. Both documents root catechesis fully in a Revelation-based approach and insist that catechesis is a unique form of teaching quite different from any other form of teaching. Both documents place great emphasis on catechesis as transmission — the respectful handing on of a deposit of faith that we have received from Christ, the Apostles, and the living Magisterium of the Church.

The Catechism

The *Catechism* (CCC), by giving a complete and integrated presentation of the faith, remedies one of the major deficiencies of past decades in catechesis — minimalization of doctrinal content, omission of certain doctrines, psychologizing of content, and one-sided treatment of certain topics.

The *Catechism* was especially driven by two concerns that surfaced at the Synod of Bishops in 1985 that gave rise to the proposal for a *Catechism*:

1. Unity in faith: this imperative is as old as the Church — as St. Paul said — "Make every effort to preserve the unity which has the Spirit as its origin and peace as its binding force. There is but one body and one Spirit, just as there is but one hope given all of you by your call. There is one Lord, one faith, one baptism; one God and Father of all, who is over all, and works through all and is in all" (Eph 4:4-6). Now at the service of this "one faith" there exists a *Catechism* to give all members of the human family a common language with which to express and celebrate it.

2. Faith as organic: in the post-conciliar period, there seemed to be a certain fragmentation of the faith, subtle omissions, exaggerations of some aspects, neglect of others. The faith, however, is interdependent — the Creed leads to worship and sacraments. Morality and prayer then are a response to what God does for us in salvation history and liturgy. Therefore the CCC declares "this catechism aims at presenting an organic synthesis of the essential and fundamental concepts of Catholic doctrine" (CCC 11). These four aspects of Christian life are inseparably linked and so the four parts of the *Catechism* which elaborate them are intrinsically united.

The Directory

The new *General Directory for Catechesis* (GDC) helps to consolidate the legitimate insights of five decades of catechetical renewal — the principle of human development, respect for growth in stages of faith maturity, appropriate pedagogical methodology truly adapted to the level being taught, integration of social doctrine, emphasis on praxis, etc. It places all of these pedagogical elements, however, in a much stronger evangelization framework, building on but greatly expanding themes first laid out in the *Directory* of 1971.

The first *General Catechetical Directory* of 1971 was part of the post-conciliar process of ecclesial reform and renewal launched by the Second Vatican Council. In its Decree on Bishops, *Christus Dominus*, the Council gave renewed emphasis to the bishops' teaching and catechetical responsibilities (nos. 12-14).

The Decree noted: "The bishops should present Christian doctrine in a manner adopted to the needs of the times; that is to say, in a manner corresponding to the difficulties and problems by which people are most burdened and troubled. They should also guard that doctrine, teaching the faithful to defend and spread it" (no. 13). As an effective instrument to aid the bishops in fulfilling these exhortations, the Decree stipulated that a "*Directory* should be composed with respect to the catechetical instruction of the Christian people and should deal with the fundamental principles of such instruction, its arrangement, and the composition of books on the subject" (no. 44). The 1971 *General Catechetical Directory*'s chief influence in the ensuing two and a half decades may be found especially in three areas:

1. It rooted and situated catechesis more clearly in the broader context of the Ministry of the Word and evangelization. It rescued catechetics from any tendency to narrow indoctrination or sterile polemics.

The emphasis in the 1971 *Directory* on the evangelization dimension of catechesis preceded Pope Paul VI's Apostolic Exhortation on Evangelization by almost five years. Nonetheless, it raised the issue of the inter-relationship between catechesis and evangelization in paragraph number eighteen, noting that given today's cultural context "evangelization can precede or accompany the work of catechesis proper. In every case one must keep in mind that the element of conversion is always present in the dynamics of faith, and for that reason any form of catechesis must also perform the role of evangelization."

Certainly here the *General Catechetical Directory* was sowing the seeds of emphasis that were to be later greatly expanded on in Pope John Paul II's Apostolic Exhortation on Catechesis, *Catechesi Tradendae,* in which our Holy Father notes: "In catechetical practice the initial evangelization has often not taken place.... This means that 'catechesis' must often concern itself not only with nourishing and teaching the faith, but also with arousing it increasingly with the help of grace, with opening the heart, with converting, and with preparing total adherence to Jesus Christ on the part of those who are still on the threshold of the faith. This concern will, in part, decide the tone, the language and the method of catechesis" (*Catechesi Tradendae,* no. 19). This wise pastoral injunction of the Holy Father must be kept in mind in implementing the new *General Directory for Catechesis.*

2. The 1971 *General Catechetical Directory* for the first time in an official catechetical document also acknowledged the important reality of "spiritual development" in those who are to be catechized. Indeed, the *Directory* devoted all of Part Five to this theme, noting that certain kinds of instruction are appropriate to various stages of the education cycle: childhood, adolescence, early adulthood and adulthood.

The *General Catechetical Directory* emphasized that catechesis is not a matter of merely indoctrinating young children, but a lifelong process of faith development in which the light of the Gospel is cast on human life with its various challenges at different points in the life journey. In Chapter VIII *Sharing the Light of Faith: National Catechetical Directory for Catholics in the United States* (hereafter the *National Catechetical Directory)* highlights the link between faith and human development and the various stages through which people will normally pass in their life and faith journeys. This emphasis on catechesis as a lifelong activity for faith development has had significant influence on the development of textbooks and teacher manuals by the various catechetical publishers.

3. The 1971 *General Catechetical Directory* said some important things about content and method in catechesis that have had a significant impact and which in some ways may be seen as the harbinger for the new *Catechism of the Catholic Church*. It attempted to keep the method of catechetics appropriate to its unique revealed content.

Part Three of the *General Catechetical Directory* on the Christian message gave a sound doctrinal foundation for the methodology of catechesis and provided unifying themes by highlighting the Christocentrism of Catechesis (no. 40) and the Trinitarian Theocentrism of Catechesis (no. 41). As we will note later, these become central themes in the *Catechism of the Catholic Church.*

The revised *General Directory for Catechesis* of 1997 restates all these themes. In its own words, it aims at securing "a balance between two principal requirements":

— on the one hand the contextualization of catechesis in evangelization as envisaged by *Evangelii Nuntiandi;*
— on the other, the appropriation of the content of the faith as presented in the *Catechism of the Catholic Church* (GDC 7).

11

The Preface to the 1997 *Directory* notes new factors that have had a positive influence on catechesis: "the evangelizing vigor of the original ecclesial community has in some ways re-emerged . . . a renewal of interest in the teaching of the Fathers . . . a return to the catechumenate." The Preface rightly notes that "The Rite of Christian Initiation of Adults has proved especially useful for catechetical renewal." This is certainly borne out in the experience of the Church in the United States, where each year tens of thousands of catechumens and candidates participate in this liturgical-catechetical process of becoming members of the Catholic Church.

The new *Directory* seeks to encourage catechesis to fully exploit its evangelizing and catechumenal and inculturating dimensions for a more dynamic and vital way of presenting the faith.

According to the new *Directory*, the evangelization dimension reminds catechists that, like Jesus, the first evangelizer, they are proclaiming and teaching a "Gospel" which means "Good News." It is a message of salvation and hope based on God's love. It corresponds to the deepest need of every human heart for ultimate love and fulfillment (read especially GDC, Chapters 1 and 2).

The catechumenal dimension helps catechists to unify their teaching effort with the Church's life of worship and with a strong sense of belonging to a fellowship of believers — the Church. Catechesis must never be divorced from worship or fail to foster a strong consciousness of Church community (read especially GDC, Chapter 3).

The inculturating dimension of catechesis alerts catechists to be sensitive to the audience and situation in which they are presenting the message. The Incarnation itself is the prime model of inculturation — the Gospel must be brought to the very heart of culture and cultures, not always an easy task and one requiring careful discernment (read especially GDC, Chapter 5).

The *Catechism* and the *Directory* together now enable catechists to enter the Third Millennium with greater clarity and confidence and to serve the teaching mission entrusted by Christ to His Church with greater effectiveness. It is a promising and exciting time in which the "new evangelization" offers many rich possibilities for catechesis.

As we greet the new millennium, and as we experience the dizzying pace of rapid change in technology, communications, medicine, transportation and much more, catechists need to be reminded that there is one thing that does not change: The Creed. That is why the *Catechism* makes the Creed the first of its four pillars — all else depends on this.

This basic prayer of Christianity, the Creed, is then the framework for catechesis. It is taught and proclaimed now with the same joy and confidence as it was in the early Christian community two thousand years ago. The Creed is so central and basic because it expresses the great plan of God for the human family which He has realized in the world through the sending of the Son and the Holy Spirit.

The Creed, prayed by us, is our acknowledgment and acceptance of this wonderful divine plan. The very fact that we are celebrating the Third Millennium is humanity's acknowledgment that the coming of the Son of God two thousand years ago proclaimed in the Creed was the chief turning point of history — as the Scriptures put it, "the fullness of time" (Gal 4:4).

The most important task for catechesis then is to foster an understanding of the divine plan of revelation which has made known to us "the mystery hidden from ages and from generations past. . .; it is Christ in you, the hope for glory" (Col 1:26, 27); the divine plan of salvation for all mankind, for the whole of human history.

How wonderful then is "the mystery we proclaim." St. Paul powerfully lays out God's loving plan for humanity in his letter to the Ephesians:

As he chose us in him [Christ], before the foundation of the world, to be holy and without blemish before

13

him. In love he destined us for adoption to himself through Jesus Christ, in accord with the favor of his will, for the praise of the glory of his grace that he granted us in the beloved. In him we have redemption by his blood, the forgiveness of transgressions, in accord with the riches of his grace that he lavished upon us. In all wisdom and insight, he has made known to us the mystery of his will in accord with his favor that he set forth in him as a plan for the fullness of times. . . (1:4-10).

Discussion Questions

1. What were the concerns that led to the decision for a *Catechism of the Catholic Church*?

2. How have you found that your use of the *Catechism* addresses these concerns? How have you personally found the *Catechism* helpful in your service as a catechist?

3. The *General Directory for Catechesis* emphasizes evangelization as a chief challenge for the catechist. How do you understand this? How do you try to evangelize those you teach?

4. How has the catechumenate model affected your approach to catechesis?

Chapter 2

Four Frameworks
for Modern Catechesis

To effectively transmit the faith in the spirit of the *Catechism* and the *Directory*, religious educators must be sensitive to four frameworks that strongly affect the catechetical ministry today: the cultural, epistemological, theological, and spiritual.

Here we can only offer a few thoughts on each framework and suggest avenues for further research. The *Catechism of the Catholic Church* deals with some of these presuppositions of catechesis with great clarity in the very important first section of Part One (nos. 26-197) which is an essential background reading for the whole of the *Catechism* and a section that should be central to catechist training and frequently reread by those in this ministry. In the context of a teacher train-

15

ing course, each of these following frameworks ought to be the subject of special attention.

1. The Cultural Framework

Pope John Paul II, in *Catechesi Tradendae,* said: "We can say of catechesis, as well as evangelization in general, that it is called to bring the power of the Gospel into the very heart of culture and cultures" (no. 53). The faith that we teach is not some abstract, other-worldly system that is a refuge from the stresses of real life. The faith rather is to shed light on real human life in the actual situations in which one must be a believer in the Third Millennium.

The new *General Directory for Catechesis* asserts: "The Word of God became man, a concrete man, in space and time and rooted in a specific culture: 'Christ by his incarnation committed himself to the particular social and cultural circumstances of the men among whom he lived.' This is the original 'inculturation' of the word of God and is the model of the evangelization by the Church [AG 10; cf. AG 22a]" (GDC 109).[1]

The catechist must then be especially sensitive to the real life situation of those who are taught. In the current American scene, this poses many challenges. The culture in which we live is secular, pluralistic, and materialistic. All of this poses a great challenge to the catechist. It requires patience and understanding, especially with young people whose lives have been formed in great part by this culture and who may initially seem to be indifferent or resistant to the values and truths we teach.

One widely read American author has even spoken of the Culture of Disbelief.[2] He argues that the legal separation of Church and State in the United States has been interpreted in a way to marginalize religion altogether. It requires "the religiously faithful to act publicly and sometimes privately as well, as though their faith does not matter." Those we teach are greatly effected by this cultural framework in which they

16

must live. They, too, come to believe that faith is a strictly private and personal matter and should, for example, have no influence on our public life. Tragically, this has led many American Catholic politicians into a public policy approach totally divorced from their religious faith.

An even more troubling cultural aspect of our times is what Pope John Paul II calls "a conspiracy against life" resulting in a "culture of death." The traditional dignity of every human person is today greatly challenged by many assaults on life, unjust distribution of world resources, proliferation of armaments, ecological dangers, promotion of contraception and abortion, fostering of "assisted suicide," etc. The writings of the present Holy Father give both a trenchant cultural analysis and a reasoned response.[3]

Sensitivity to the cultural context of catechetics in the American scene must also recognize that the Church in the United States is multi-cultural. In recent decades newer waves of immigrants of Hispanic or Asian origin have enriched our parish life. At the same time, African-American and native American Catholics are legitimately seeking to express their faith in forms that are congenial to their traditions. The catechist needs to be open to and sensitive to these aspects of the cultural context of catechesis.

Finally, the *General Directory for Catechesis* gives us the broad principle that must undergird all efforts at inculturation in catechesis: "In the light of the Gospel, the Church must appropriate all the positive values of culture and of cultures [Cf. EN 20; CT 53] and reject those elements which impede development of the true potential of persons and peoples" (GDC 21).

The words of Francis Cardinal George, Archbishop of Chicago, are helpful here:

> Creating a culture which provides a more evangeli-
> cally authentic environment for daily life in the United
> States is less a program with clearly defined stages

than a movement of gradual growth. Cultural change is slow; but it can be steady if our purpose is clear and our nerves are strong. Evangelizers need a broad vision and strength for the long haul. Evangelizing culture relies on deep insight into the mysteries of our faith and keen vision for understanding the bases of our culture. Evangelizing culture is, finally, a contemplative activity. The dialogue between Catholic faith and American culture takes place in the media, in the schools and the marketplace, and in the public square; but it begins in the heart of every American Catholic who loves both faith and country.[4]

2. The Epistemological Framework

Catechesis involves teaching and learning in order to come to know God's Word. This philosophical term — epistemology — refers to how we know anything. It has important implications for the catechists. Our ordinary human knowledge involves a process of "data collection" through the senses, with input from the imagination and the memory, and by exercising our reasoning powers to make sense of the data we have received. It often leads to convictions and judgments.

The Church has always been a defender of human reason and the wonderful possibilities of the human intelligence. Most recently Pope John Paul II in his encyclical letter on faith and reason underlined how every human being is in a way a philosopher — that he seeks to know the meaning of his own existence.

There are, however, three problems concerning the ideal process of knowing, described above, to which the catechist must be alert. First, our feelings can cloud and distort the process. Feelings are emotions that arise from a variety of sources — physiological, environmental, upbringing, life experience, reaction to other persons, etc. Feelings in themselves are generally neutral, neither good or bad. They are usually the spontaneous response to a stimulus of some kind. They can become harmful and sinful if we deliberately act on them in an inappropriate way: giving in to unjust anger; compulsions in eating, drinking; inappropriate sexual behavior, etc.

Modern people, however, especially young people, confuse knowing and feeling. They often act on their feelings without a process of reasoning. There is much in our culture that fosters this as we have noted earlier. It leads to a very superficial and shallow personality, lack of character and conviction, and tragically often to self-destructive behavior.

Religious educators, therefore, must be clear about epistemology — how we know truth — and be able to help those they serve to more carefully differentiate their reason and feelings. This is especially basic for any successful moral catechesis.

A second problem in the area of knowing is that all the elements of our knowing process have been wounded by the effects of original sin. Our mind is clouded and cannot always easily attain truth; our will is weakened and cannot always easily make proper decisions. This realistic anthropology is important for religious educators to take into account in the ministry of catechesis. As the *Catechism* reminds us:

In the historical conditions in which he finds himself, however, man experiences many difficulties in coming to know God by the light of reason alone:

Though human reason is, strictly speaking, truly capable by its own natural power and light of attaining to a true and certain knowledge of the one personal God, who watches over and controls the world by his providence, and of the natural law written in our hearts by the Creator; yet there are many obstacles which prevent reason from the effective and fruitful use of this inborn faculty. For the truths that concern the relations between God and man wholly transcend the visible order of things, and, if they are translated into human action and influence it, they call for self-surrender and abnegation. The human mind, in its turn, is hampered in the attaining of such truths, not only by the impact of the senses and the imagination, but also by disordered appetites which are the consequences of original sin. So it happens that men in such matters easily persuade themselves that what they would not like to be true is false or at least doubtful [Pius XII, *Humani Generis*, 561; DS 3875] (CCC 37).

A third problem is that while human reasoning processes can theoretically lead us to a certain knowledge of the existence of an Infinite Being, they cannot by themselves lead us to a knowledge of the Trinity or the divine plan. The human mind is locked within the possibilities of the merely human and so cannot bring us to the most important truths about the divine plan and purpose. I believe it may indeed be true, as some theologians maintain, that there is in our nature an "unrestricted drive towards the transcendent" that creates an opening for God that nothing human can ever satisfy. This would be fitting since the author of creation and redemption is the one God and has intended from all eternity His human creatures to be in a relationship of love with Himself. Nevertheless this potency does not lead to the knowledge of God's nature or purpose which are beyond unaided human observation.

This last problem then leads us logically to the next framework needed for the catechist's task — the theological framework.

3. The Theological Framework

Both the *Catechism of the Catholic Church* and the *General Directory for Catechesis* insist that catechesis be Revelation-based. The directive may be confusing to some catechists who in recent years were encouraged to see catechesis as "human experience based." It is crucial then to listen to the rationale these two documents give for a Revelation-based catechesis which gives the true theological context for catechesis. The *Catechism of the Catholic Church* states:

> By natural reason man can know God with certainty, on the basis of his works. But there is another order of knowledge, which man cannot possibly arrive at by his own powers: the order of divine Revelation [Cf. *Dei Filius*: DS 3015]. Through an utterly free decision, God has revealed himself and given himself to man. This he does by revealing the mystery, his plan of loving goodness, formed from all eternity in Christ, for the benefit of all men. God has fully revealed this plan by sending us his beloved Son, our Lord Jesus Christ, and the Holy Spirit (CCC 50).

It is important for catechists to have a clear understanding of Divine Revelation. Our mass culture often relegates religion to the realm of sentiment or feelings and thus reduces it to a totally subjective reality.

The Christian conviction, however, is that the truths of faith are not produced by the human mind but are revealed to us by the free initiative of a loving God who wants to bring us into a relationship of intimacy with Himself.

As a human relationship grows in mutual self-disclosure motivated by love, as for instance between an engaged couple, so God out of love reveals Himself to us to draw us ever closer to Himself, to actually adopt us as sons and daughters into the divine family of the Trinity.

So it happened that as the letter to the Hebrews puts it: "In times past, God spoke in fragmentary and varied ways to our fathers through the prophets; in this, the final age, he has spoken to us through his Son" (Heb 1:1).

The Incarnation of the Eternal Son is the culmination of Revelation. Jesus, in His person, is the very "image of God"

(2 Cor 4:4) for us. By His teaching and by His deeds He has revealed to us what no human could otherwise know about God and His purpose: "No one knows the Father except the Son and anyone to whom the Son wishes to reveal him" (Mt 11:27). Divine Revelation therefore constitutes the essential theological framework for catechesis — it provides us with the mystery and content that we are to transmit. It comes to us from God and is received in faith (read especially GCD [*General Catechetical Directory*], Chapter 1, 36-42; CCC 50-73).

This realization can bring the catechist great security and confidence. It is not a question primarily of the personality or skills of the catechist that makes their efforts fruitful, but rather their faithfulness to transmitting faithfully the Word of God as they have received it from the Church. The "Good News" faithfully transmitted has its own power to touch hearts and minds.

Human experience has a significant role to play in catechesis which will be developed more fully in part five of this book on the Methodology of Catechesis but it is not a substitute for a Revelation-based approach. The ultimate source for catechesis is the Word of God transmitted by Divine Revelation. As the *General Catechetical Directory* puts it:

The source from which catechesis draws its message is the word of God: "Catechesis will always draw its content from the living source of the word of God transmitted in Tradition and the Scriptures, for sacred Tradition and the sacred Scripture make up a single sacred deposit of the word of God, which is entrusted to the Church [CT 27]."

"This deposit of faith" [Cf. DV 10 a e b; cf: 1 Tim 6:20 and 2 Tim 1:14] is like the treasure of a householder; it is entrusted to the Church, the family of God, and she continuously draws from it things new and old [Cf. Mt 13:52]. All God's children, animated by his Spirit, are nourished by this treasure of the Word" (GCD 94).

4. The Spirituality Framework

One of the most significant teachings of the Second Vatican Council is contained in the Constitution on the Church, Chapter V, "The Universal Call to Holiness."

Trying to respond to a widespread presumption that real holiness was a goal best left to monks, nuns, or priests, the Council declared:

> It is quite clear that all Christians in any state or walk of life are called to the fullness of Christian life and to the perfection of love, and by this holiness a more human manner of life is fostered also in earthly society. . . . This holiness is shown forth in the fruits of grace which the Spirit produces in the faithful; it is expressed in many ways by the individuals, who each in his own state of life, tend to the perfection of love (no. 39).

The Council, of course, was only recapturing the most ancient Biblical teaching as Yahweh spoke to His people: "Be holy for I, the Lord your God, am holy" (Lev 19:2). Jesus made this the centerpiece of His teaching: "You must be made perfect as your heavenly Father is perfect" (Mt 5:48).

The *Catechism*, building on this scriptural and conciliar teaching, alerts catechists that their task is not only to communicate knowledge about God but is to help those they serve to truly live lives based on this teaching. Spirituality is not an esoteric search for inner refreshment but it is in the words of Book Three of the *Catechism*: "Life in Christ."

This "mystery we proclaim" includes the truth that by Baptism we are incorporated into Christ as members to a body or branches to a vine. We live by Christ's life. Every Christian can re-echo Paul's powerful words, "I live now — no longer I — but Christ lives in me." Spirituality is about how we live and express this life of Christ in us.

The chief agent of growth in holiness is the Holy Spirit. It is the Spirit who enables us to call the Infinite God — "Abba"/ My Father (Gal 4:7) and to call Jesus "Lord" (1 Cor 12:3). It is the Spirit who gives us those gifts and fruits that enable us to reflect the Christ life within us (Gal 5:22). It is the Spirit who strengthens us in our weakness (Rom 8:26). Catechists should be certain that those they instruct understand the role and power of this often neglected person of the Most Blessed Trinity.

Book Three of the *Catechism* tells the catechist that this spirituality has to be based on the Beatitudes (Mt 5:3-12) taught by Christ and be expressed in a life of virtue. In the Beatitudes is found "the goal of human existence" as "God calls us to his own beatitude" (CCC 1719). God calls each individual and the whole Church, which is all of the people who accept his promise and live it in faith. "A virtue is a habitual and firm disposition to do the good. It allows the person not only to perform good acts, but to give the best of himself. The virtuous person tends toward the good with all his sensory and spiritual powers; he pursues the good and chooses it in concrete actions. The goal of a virtuous life is to become like God" (CCC 1803).

Book Four of the *Catechism* on Christian prayer is an addition to the former traditional *Catechism* framework of Creed, sacraments, and Commandments. The decision to add this fourth part reflects the Conciliar consciousness that all are called to holiness and therefore, all need instruction on the means to grow in holiness. Paramount among the means, after the sacraments treated in Book Two, is prayer, treated in Book Four. Catechists need, above all, to help those they serve to develop a faithful daily practice of prayer to enable them to grow in Christian holiness.

Discussion Questions

1. Cultural Framework — What aspects of American culture do you find most hostile to the Christian message? Do young people understand the ways in which they are influ-

enced and manipulated by the popular culture? How can we help them to be "countercultural"?

2. Epistemological Framework — Do your students make a distinction between reason and feelings? Are their actions more motivated by feelings than Gospel values?

3. Theological Framework — How do you understand "Revelation"? Why is it such an important idea for catechesis?

4. Spiritual Framework — What does spirituality mean to you? How can you help students grow in a Christian way of life? What prayer opportunities do you provide with your catechesis?

Notes

1. For an excellent analysis of issues of evangelization and inculturation see, Francis Cardinal George, "Evangelizing American Culture" in the *New Catholic Evangelization*, ed. by K. Boyack (New York: Paulist Press, 1992).

2. Stephen Carter, *The Culture of Disbelief: How American Law and Politics Trivialize Religion* (New York: Doubleday & Co., 1994).

3. See especially John Paul VI, "The Gospel of Life," 1995 and "The Splendor of Truth," 1993. While these two papal Encyclicals can be challenging reading for the catechist, they are a brilliant and reasoned response to some of the chief moral issues of our time.

4. Op. cit. George, *New Catholic Evangelization*, p. 53.

Part Two
The Heritage and the Challenge

Chapter 1

Historical Context

We are approaching the Third Millennium of Christianity. For believers, this is a meaningful milestone in the trajectory from the first appearance of the Son of God on this earth to His glorious second and final appearance. This in-between time is the "era of the Church." It is a time of mission, evangelization, proclamation, and invitation in which every believer should be involved. In this context, catechesis has a central role to play in the Church's mission.

The historical benchmark of A.D. 2000 in this "era of the Church" is a fitting time to reassess our catechetical efforts, to see where we have come from and what challenges we still face. The Second Vatican Council asserted: "At all times the Church carries the responsibility of reading the signs of the time and of interpreting them in the light of the Gospel."[1] Perhaps this injunction is more urgent then ever as we approach the Third Millennium. There are many indications that this can be a moment of great opportunity for the Church and its mission. The demise of anti-religious totalitarian regimes in the East and the emergence of unsatisfied spiritual hunger in the West offer a *kairos* — a privileged moment — for renewed evangelization and catechetics.

Where Have We Been?

It may be helpful to review, briefly, the phases of the catechetical renewal through which we have passed — trends which have so influenced the way the faith is taught today in the Catholic Church in the United States.[2] We can then look to the future and to the challenges it holds for the catechetical ministry. The focus of catechesis in the early centuries of Christianity was clearly on forming vibrant, adult faith communities. In those times of frequent and brutal persecution, the commitment required to embrace and practice the faith often bordered on the heroic. The level of commitment is reflected in the centuries of conflict over how to deal with the "lapsi" — those who, in face of persecution, either denied or feigned a denial of the faith. Furthermore, entrance into the early faith community was not casual; it involved a lengthy and demanding catechumenate.

In the Middle Ages, Columban monks from Ireland undertook the evangelization of Northern Europe. The faith witness of the monks and the establishment of their monastic centers incorporated these peoples into the community of faith. Benedictine monks built upon their ministry by helping the nomadic peoples to adopt a settled farming economy and to acquire the rudiments of education. Most importantly, they also deepened their faith understanding and commitment.

Medieval Christians enjoyed a visual catechesis in cathedral environments. A series of festivals, folk celebrations, and mystery and morality plays also vividly involved them in the celebration of the mysteries of Christ.

Counter-Reformation Catholics responded to the Protestant challenge by developing a strong doctrinal catechesis. It used a set question-and-answer method whose clarity and precision was an effective response for the times. (See Appendix for detailed outline of the stages of catechetical developments.)

The Jesuits augmented this academic exercise with catechetical dramas based on the Gospel stories. Philip Neri invited the musicians of Rome — especially Palestrina — to put the Gospel dialogues to music. These works were performed in his Oratory, giving rise to the oratorio art form so effectively developed by Bach and Händel.

The catechism of the Council of Trent established a classic pattern of Creed, Code, and Cult for transmitting the content of the faith. This has been recaptured in the universal catechism of Vatican II, and the approach is harmonious with that of the ancient catechumenate.

Many adaptations of the Trent catechism were developed in different countries. The Baltimore Catechism appeared in the United States in 1885 and, in various versions, was widely used until the post-World War II period.

The Modern Catechetical Renewal

At the turn of the twentieth century, efforts to find a catechetical method more effective than the traditional question-answer approach began with the so-called Munich Method. This included educational strategies of presentation, explanation, and application of the catechetical content. This approach, it was felt, corresponded to the steps in the learning process: perception, understanding, and practice. It would engage all the faculties of the student — not just the intellect.

The second major development of the modern catechetical renewal involved the actual content. It was sparked by the Austrian Jesuit Joseph Jungmann, and the publication in 1937 of his landmark book *The Good News: Yesterday and Today.*[3]

Jungmann called on the Church to recapture the dynamism of its primitive, Christocentric kerygma as the focus of catechetical content, rather than the abstract scholastic language that characterized the existing catechism. He also reintroduced the concept of "salvation history" as expressing the great sweep of God's redeeming plan, unfolding through four thousand years of God's self-revelation, beginning with Abraham and looking forward to culmination in the Parousia. The content of catechesis was also affected by a renewed focus on evangelization as Europe saw its Catholic character eroding. The writings of persons such as Emmanuel Cardinal Suhard and Canon Joseph Cardijn were reinforced by the reflections of those catechizing in missionary lands. These theological trends culminated in the Apostolic Exhortation on Evangelization[4] of Pope Paul VI, finding structural embodiment in the promulgation of the revised Rite for Christian Initiation of Adults (RCIA).

The third major development of the modern catechetical renewal was the influence of modern developmental psychology. The research and insights of psychologists such as Piaget, Kohlberg, and Fowler were accepted, sometimes uncritically, by religious educators and publishers. On balance, this has been a positive development, endorsed in the *National Catechetical Directory* by an entire chapter titled "Catechesis Toward Maturity in Faith."[5] Pope John Paul II, in *Catechesi Tradendae*, has utilized this principle with exquisite pastoral sensitivity in his suggestions regarding content appropriate for various stages of human growth.[6]

This development is one factor that has helped to refocus attention and energy on the catechesis of adults. It points to the norm of the mature, adult believer as the goal of youth catechesis, and identifies the stages of adult change cycles with their special religious needs and possibilities.

Furthermore, developmental psychology has encouraged catechesis to use inductive and life-issue-oriented approaches to bridge the gap between faith and life. Occasionally, however, this development led to an anthropocentric focus in which catechesis was reduced to a species of "pop psychology."

A fourth major phase of the modern catechetical renewal, one still in progress, might be called its prophetic phase. The content now includes the implications of the Gospel for societal renewal, for justice, charity, and peace among groups and nations. The consciousness-raising educational methodology of pioneers such as Paolo Freire has been applied to religious education by writers such as Thomas Groome[7] and are greatly influencing catechesis, especially in Latin America.

The history of catechesis represented by these phases of the catechetical renewal puts in the hands of the modern religious educator many of the tools (scriptural, educational, theological, psychological) needed to effectively address today's context and to meet its challenges.

Cultural Shifts and Seductions

We have undergone a major cultural shift in this century, and it has left a profound impact on society and therefore on the Church. It is pastorally crucial to acknowledge and accept this changed sociocultural context for catechesis and to see it as a pastoral challenge.

Some traditionalists refuse to do this and wish to freeze the Church in the brief moment of its journey which they believe is non-native. This may give momentary comfort and security to a few persons, but it is not the true way of the Church, which exists for the evangelization of the real world and its people.

The Holy Spirit given by Christ to the Church is its dynamic principle of life, enabling it to faithfully proclaim the perennial "Good News" to every culture and in every period of history. The new sociocultural situation needs to be faced with tranquillity and with a spirit of discernment. As in the past, it is filled with positive and negative factors, opportunities, and perils.

We should see this contemporary situation as a life-giving challenge to pastoral creativity. We need to analyze its dimensions and realistically imagine how the ancient faith can be effectively proclaimed and taught in the real situation that confronts us as we move toward the Third Millennium of Christianity.

Commentators propose different reasons for the new cultural situation in which the Church must now function; e.g., the rise of cities, the Protestant Reformation, the Enlightenment, the Kantian "turn to the subject," the modern emergence of scientific empiricism, the Industrial Age, the modern democratic movements, the technological revolution.

All of these movements certainly are contributing factors in shaping the modern world and mentality. A detailed analysis of each would be beyond the scope of this book. However, the end result of all these complex factors is that modern culture and thinking are characterized by strong currents of subjectivism, individualism, relativism, pragmatism, and materialism.

Modern subjectivism, for instance, believes that the human person alone (and often his or her feelings alone) must be the ultimate criteria of decision. Personhood often means self-achievement. There is often a consequent denial (theoretical or practical) that there is a Transcendent Absolute which is the source and destiny of human existence. Accordingly, there is no universally accepted philosophy of human nature or human society.

Modern relativism leads many persons to consider all assertions as "opinion." People speak of "my truth" or "your truth" as if all statements were of equal validity — even contradictory ones. An objective truth which transcends personal opinion or feeling is a difficult reality for many moderns to accept. Consequently a major cultural value has become "tolerance," in which a vast pluralism of views can be allowed to coexist. In such a climate the Gospel adage "you shall know the truth and the truth shall set you free" (Jn 8:32) is problematic.

32

Influenced by these trends, secular education has often taken either pragmatic or ideological directions.[8] On the pragmatic side, it has been seen less as a means to learn the history and culture of the human race and more as preparation for pragmatic employment. On the theoretical side, it has sometimes degenerated into a cacophony of competing "politically correct" ideologies designed to bolster the self-esteem of some group that feels left out of the allegedly white male Eurocentric form of education.

A major result of all these tendencies has been the uncritical acceptance of a limitless pluralism in the face of which one is hesitant to assert any truths as objective, certain, and normative for thought and behavior. The contemporary glorification of pluralism obviously creates a difficulty for the transmission of Christian truth, which is oriented toward leading people precisely to "the obedience of faith" (Rom 1:5).

Changing Ecclesial Context

Not only has the cultural context for catechesis changed, but the ecclesial context has also changed. Some of these changes have been noted above in the brief history of the phases of the modern catechetical renewal earlier in Chapter One.

The Church's theology has been greatly influenced by the shift from the classical intellectual approach to a more historical and process-oriented approach. Pastorally, Church life has been effected by the impetus given by the Second Vatican Council to a renewed liturgy, a greater sense of the universal call to holiness, and participation in the Church's mission, a keener appreciation of the relevance of the Church's message to the social-justice issues of the modern world. All of these developments bring new emphases and priorities which also must be part of the new context for religious education.

The immediate context of catechetical service for most of our readers is the Catholic Church in the United States. The studies of sociologists have shown that the American-Catholic cultural ghetto is disappearing and that Catholics are now fully in the mainstream of American life. In their book *The American Catholic People*, authors Gallup and Castelli describes a "two-tier" Catholic community which is the context for catechetical efforts. They note: "American Catholics have developed a stunning momentum — economically, socially, politically, spiritually — that ensures that they will have a profound impact on the shape of American society." They also observe that we are growing — the percentage of Americans who call themselves Catholic has grown by almost half in forty years, and they predict that "somewhere in the middle of the next century, Catholics would vie with Protestants as the dominant religion in America."[9]

The percentage of Catholics with a college background has more than doubled in the past twenty years and is constantly increasing. In addition, our income level has grown substantially. These kinds of upscale, professional, educated people are the ones whose educational needs as adults the parish must try to meet with sophisticated programs of evangelization, adult education, and faith nurture.

Yet precisely their affluence has often created a spiritual vacuum that makes it difficult to engage or interest them in programs of adult religious education in any great numbers. Their upward mobility often makes them indifferent or even hostile to the challenges of the Gospel message about social justice. It was precisely our most affluent Catholics who organized the most vocal protest to the American Bishops' pastoral letter on the economy.

The impact of this changing nature of our constituents has also had its impact on Catholic schools. Some, feeling newly liberated from their former immigrant convictions, unfairly devalue Catholic schools as narrow or anti-American. Others value the schools for inadequate reasons. They prize the academic and disciplinary achievements of our schools more than the religious and spiritual goals which give them their ultimate meaning. These parents have bought into the

American dream of economic success and want their children prepared to achieve high SAT scores for college more than any spiritual development.

In the other tier, the lower economic level is also filled with Catholics to be served. In many ways we are still very much an immigrant Church. Hispanics make up at least 16 percent of American Catholics; three percent are black, and three percent are Asian. I am told that the Eucharist is offered in more different languages in some United States dioceses on a weekend than probably anywhere on earth! These immigrant families still look to the Church for major support in their struggles and for hope for their children's education and religious growth.

The impact that this has on our parish catechetical programs is great. Many of these people are not accustomed to regimented once-a-week religion classes. Religious education is natural and deeply rooted in the family; it finds colorful expression in feasts and devotions which the suburban American no longer finds appealing. How do the Church and the parish respond and serve both groups with an effective catechetical program?

A Result: Cultural Catholicism?

For both the second- and third-generation Catholic and the newer arrivals, the cultural and sociological supports for faith practice which greatly forged Catholic identity and loyalty in the past have eroded.

The danger now is that instead of clear Catholic identity based on true ecclesial and doctrinal foundations, a rather loose sociocultural Catholic identity will be retained. This Catholic identity may be without clear commitment to authentic Catholic faith or moral teachings but more in the line of a cultural affiliation based on ancestry or family tradition.

The secular media have in fact already trumpeted the emergence of "cultural Catholics." A *New York Times* piece announced that "Cultural Catholics Take an Independent Path"

(June 18, 1986). The article dealt with "What does it mean to be a Catholic?" and the author's disturbing report is that this new kind of Catholic not only dissents from the Church's moral teaching in significant areas but also sees the Incarnation and Resurrection as "fairy tales" which, "whether or not they are fact," at best bring a needed dimension of tradition to rootless modern life that would be otherwise lacking!

Sociologist Andrew Greeley speaks of a "new religious Consciousness" among young people by which they experience a "tender loving God" and have a very positive attitude to religious realities. Gone is the preoccupation with sin, judgment, and legalism. He optimistically prophesies: "Because of this new vision of God and of life, the New Breed is more likely to be open to Church careers, more socially committed, more insistent in high-quality performance by the Church, more formed in their prayer, more concerned about social justice, and more personally devout."[10]

However, experienced religious educators, in daily contact with young people, have another perspective. William J. O'Malley acknowledges a "radical change in our image of God" that is perceived by the students but attributes it to a vapid, non-biblical, overly-psychologized catechesis that has reduced Jesus to a "warm fuzzy." Such a caricature leads young people to believe that the Lord "seems to want nothing more than that we 'be not afraid' and let him take care of everything," that God is basically "a pushover."[11]

James DiGiacomo strokes a similar warning note. He believes that the impact of the self-absorbed culture and much inadequate catechesis has been to produce in young people "a new illiteracy" with regard not just to the information content of the faith but to its most basic and fundamental concepts — the nature of conversion and repentance, sin and redemption, and the moral challenges of an authentic Christian life. He makes a significant observation when he writes: "The short-comings of youthful religious belief and practice are a function of a crisis of identity in the larger community."[12]

36

However we evaluate these various perceptions of contemporary American and ecclesial life, our approach to catechesis must take realistic stock of the changed context in which we seek to proclaim the ancient faith. We must strive to examine the "signs of the times" to determine how to develop a language, signs, and symbols that can faithfully but convincingly bring the Church's faith to the modern world!

As this observer looks at some of our catechetical efforts in recent decades, there are many causes for gratitude and satisfaction. The impact of biblical studies, theology, developmental psychology, and pedagogical sciences on catechesis have resulted in some very important and useful improvements in the content of catechesis and in our understanding of how to catechize more effectively.

Nonetheless, there are areas where our catechetical efforts could use critical evaluation and reform. I would like to list several:

1. I see too much emphasis on process and not enough on product. I am concerned that means have sometimes replaced ends. Method has overtaken the purpose of catechetics. The question "Why should I catechize?" has yielded its rightful position to "How must I catechize?" But if we cease to know where we are going, what difference does it make about what road should be taken?

Catechesis is supposed to be a road map for earthly and eternal life. It is meant to be a faith guide for conversion to Jesus, moral living, development of Christian character, and growth of spirituality in this life so that we can arrive at our divinely appointed destiny: "We shall be like him, / for we shall see him as he is" (1 Jn 3:2). I shall return to this issue when discussing the goals of catechesis in Part Two.

2. I hear too little about truth and a great deal about opinion. As I have noted, tolerance of all ideas has become a master value of our culture. This results in a relativism which assumes no truth can be affirmed. Unfortunately, the same misplaced use of tolerance has appeared in catechesis. We should

indeed be tolerant of persons and jettison all forms of prejudice against them. But tolerance should not impede our quest for truth or our confidence that it can be found.

The contemporary catechist, to be effective in a culture of conflicting views and relativism, must be strongly grounded in the truth of the faith and humbly, but confidently, be willing to share it. This is not done in any triumphalistic spirit, but as the ultimate service a believer can render to another human being.

Some catechetical theorists have written that catechesis should foster a "critical spirit" and "ambiguity." They are nervous about anything smacking of "the tyranny of linguistic orthodoxy," "dogmatism," or "triumphal ecclesiology." I believe this attitude reflects the spirit of the times more than the Gospel.

I contrast this with John Chrysostom's view of what it means to teach in Christ's name. He proposes John the Evangelist as a model, and of him he writes: "See the great boldness and power of the words, how he speaks nothing doubting or conjecturing, but declares all things plainly. For this is the teacher's part, not to waver in anything he says, since, were he, who is to be guide to the rest, to require another to establish him with certainty, would he be rightly ranked not among teachers, but among disciples."[13]

3. I sense there is a "missing person" in today's catechesis. One reads a great deal about getting in touch with the human Jesus. Yes, there is a humanity of Jesus, but it is always united to His divinity. The full mystery and power of Jesus (see Col 1:15-20) needs to be proclaimed. All people need to hear the power of the earliest Christian proclamation, "Jesus is Lord" (Rom 10:9).

What Paul VI said of evangelization is equally true of catechesis: "There is no true evangelization if the name, the teaching, the life, the promises, the Kingdom, and the mystery of Jesus of Nazareth, the Son of God, are not proclaimed."[14] Only a Christocentric catechesis that fully presents Jesus as the preexistent Word, who created all and who emptied Himself to win our salvation and now reigns as Lord of the Universe, is faithful to the full mystery of our faith.

4. I believe that catechesis has also lost some of its dynamism and impact because it has lost the power of the biblical drama of salvation. All other ages of Christianity thrived because they accepted the truths of salvation history, which included the sinful situation of human beings, the cry for a redeemer, and the gracious response of God by means of the Incarnation of His Son, Jesus Christ, who came to redeem us by His life, death, Resurrection, sending of the Spirit, and foundation of the Church.

Where, in much of contemporary catechesis, is the portrayal of a "lost humanity" as Paul preaches it?[15] Who emphasizes the centrality of Jesus for reconciliation with God? While one may find words to this effect in catechetical materials, it is rarely the master teaching around which everything is built. There is no purpose for our faith, and, therefore, for our catechesis, unless the proclamation of Jesus as Savior and source of reconciliation with God and divine life for all is not insistently and persuasively transmitted.

5. Finally, I sometimes detect an inadequate and superficial ecclesiology. Of course the Church must be incarnated in each culture of history. This does not mean changing the teachings and nature of the Church to fit the fashions of the times. Such a misguided view results from what I would call the politicizing of our understanding of the Church. Seeing the Church in political terms reduces it to partisan advocacy. It justifies pitching one wing of the Church against another. It persuades us to undermine a divinely given teaching authority and replace it with a "voters' view" of what should be believed. This is the real evil in cultural Catholicism. Catechesis in such a view becomes a political football, an indoctrination tool for partisans.

Jesus opposed the "cultural Judaism" of His time. The Body of Christ must oppose cultural Catholicism today. Jesus made it clear that His Kingdom was not of this world. In fact, only when this is understood is the Kingdom of Jesus able to bring to the cultures of this world the true justice, mercy, love, and fulfillment they seek.

The above five observations are in my mind as I write this book. There is an identity crisis in catechesis today, and I believe the issues I have cited are some of the contributing factors. Until Catholic catechesis has recovered its true purpose, it will continue to wander from one methodological fad to another and leave behind yet more religious illiteracy. Only when there is a revitalized confidence that truth can be known and that the Christian mystery embodies the ultimate truth will today's catechesis create the strong faith and witnessing communities which will be needed as we move toward A.D. 2000.

Perhaps there is at this moment of catechetical history a parallel between our experience and that of the Apostle Paul in his teaching ministry. When he taught at Athens he tried to adapt to the culture of his hearers, and therefore he had only very modest success. But when he went to Corinth he realized that he must reorganize himself. He finally understood what his catechesis must be, a religious proclamation that found all its energy and strength in the mystery of Jesus Christ, even when it was "an absurdity to Gentiles" (1 Cor 1:23). "When I came to you, brethren, I did not come proclaiming to you the testimony of God in lofty words or wisdom. For I decided to know nothing among you except Jesus Christ and him crucified" (RSV 1 Cor 2:1-2) Corinth was the turning point in Paul's catechesis. It was then that he became the effective instrument of God in bringing others to Jesus and salvation.

I believe that lifeless catechesis will recover vigor and impact when it returns to the full drama of salvation and the full mystery of Jesus Christ, "the mystery of our faith" (1 Tim 3:16). This is why I believe we need to recapture an "ecclesial" understanding of catechesis that is deeply rooted in what the Spirit has done over the centuries in the teaching Church. Catechesis is not just an alternative psychological "self-help" treatise. Faithfulness to the full mystery and message was the secret of the success of the great catechesis of the Apostles, the Fathers of the Church, the mighty contributions of a Canisius and a Bellarmine, and all of the humble but faith-filled people who taught the catechism to our immigrant parents and grandparents.

Similar faithfulness on our part will guarantee that the catechetical history we have surveyed will continue in the decades ahead to enliven the Church with enthusiasm, foster the emergence of saints, and enable the Church to witness effectively to the world.

Discussion Questions

1. In your lifetime, what are the chief changes you have experienced in catechesis — in its content? In its methods or techniques?

2. What evidence do you see of "cultural Catholicism" in your students? How can you counteract this tendency?

Notes

1. *Conciliar and Post-Conciliar Documents*, ed. by Austin Flannery, O.P. (Northport, N.Y.: Costello Publishing Co., 1975).

2. *Gaudium et Spes*, Pastoral Constitution on the Church in the Modern World, no. 4, Vatican Council II. For a fuller historical treatment, see Michael Warren, *Sourcebook for Modern Catechetics* (Winona, Minn.: St. Mary's Press, 1983), Part One, pp. 23 ff.

3. Joseph Jungmann, *The Good News: Yesterday and Today* (New York: Sadlier Publishing Co., 1962).

4. Pope Paul VI, *Evangelii Nuntiandi*, Apostolic Exhortation on Evangelization (Washington, D.C.: United States Catholic Conference, 1975).

5. *Sharing the Light of Faith: National Catechetical Directory for Catholics in the United States* (Washington, D.C.: United States Catholic Conference, 1979).

6. Pope John Paul II, *Catechesi Tradendae*, Apostolic Exhortation on Instruction and Formation in the Faith (Washington, D.C.: United States Catholic Conference, 1979), nos. 35-44.

7. Thomas Groome, *Christian Religious Education* (San Francisco: Harper and Row, 1980).

8. See Allan Bloom, *The Closing of the American Mind* (Simon & Schuster, 1987) and Dinesh D'Souza, *Illiberal Education* (New York: Macmillan Co., 1991).

9. See George Gallup and James Castelli, *The American Catholic People: Their Beliefs, Practices and Values* (New York: Doubleday & Co., 1987); *The People's Religion: American Faith in the 90s* (New York: Macmillan Co., 1989).

10. Andrew M. Greeley, "A Post-Vatican II New Breed?" *America*, June 28, 1980.

11. William J. O'Malley, S.J., "Teenager and You Know What," *America*, April 15, 1989.

12. James J. DiGiacomo, "The New Illiteracy," *Church,* Fall 1986.

13. John Chrysostom, *Homily 2 on John's Gospel*, par. 7.

14. Pope Paul VI, *Evangelii Nuntiandi*, no. 22.

15. See Romans 1:18 through 3:1-31.

Chapter 2

What Is Catechesis?

As we consider the ongoing catechetical renewal, it seems appropriate at this point to raise the basic issue about the nature of catechesis. What is catechesis? I prefer to use the term catechesis because I believe it highlights the absolutely unique ecclesial nature of this activity. Others prefer terms such as religious education, religious socialization, and Christian religious education.[1]

I believe the preferred term should be "catechesis" because it is the term the Church has historically used for this essential ministry of instruction in the faith. All who catechize do so as servants of the mission of the Church. Catechesis, therefore, is a term that removes ambivalence about the unique ecclesial nature of this ministry.

The word catechesis comes from a Greek verb that means to "reecho" — the emphasis is on transmission, the passing on of a message received. This term, I believe, best corresponds to the two-thousand-year-old experience and practice of the Church and has been recently recaptured in the Rite of Christian Initiation of Adults (RCIA).

As a simple working definition of catechesis, I would like to suggest the following: "Catechesis is the transmission of God's Word to invite people to personal faith." Transmission puts the emphasis on our listening to and acceptance of God's Word as the fundamental dynamic of catechetical ministry. This ministry is a service to God's Word and the faith of the people.

Scripture scholars tell us that one of the earliest examples of catechesis is contained in Paul's letter to the Corinthians. It is found in two places where he is teaching his converts about two of the most basic doctrines of our faith — the Resurrection and the Eucharist. How does Paul go about his teaching? Let us listen to his words so that we may find a clue for our own efforts: (a) The Resurrection: "I handed on to you first of all what I myself received, that Christ died for our sins in accordance with the Scriptures; that he was buried and, in accordance with the Scriptures, rose on the third day. . ." (1 Cor 15:3 ff.); (b) The Eucharist: "This is what I received from the Lord and what I handed on to you, namely, that the Lord Jesus on the night in which he was betrayed took bread, and after he had given thanks broke it and said 'This is my body which is for you. Do this in remembrance of me' " (1 Cor 11:23-24). Paul clearly sees himself as the servant of a truth or a doctrine that he has accepted and wishes to share.

Understanding catechesis as "the transmission of God's words to invite others to faith" not only reflects a biblical approach but also has some practical implications for our efforts as religious educators.

1. The focus is on God's Word, His Revelation, His will. We listen and learn and teach things that we could never discover by our own human intellect or reason or by any reflec-

tion on human experience. We discover the incredible love of God for us, we learn about the greatest miracle of all time — the Incarnation; we hear about our adoption as sons of God and coheirs with Christ; we learn about our destiny for "eternal glory"; we hear about the Eucharist, "our food for the journey," and about the communion of saints — the powerful friends and helpers we have on our pilgrim way: Mary, the angels, the saints. Understanding religious education in this way puts the emphasis where it should be — on the theocentric instead of the anthropocentric. God has taken the initiative. We respond with gratitude and love and obedience, what Paul calls "the obedience of faith" (Rom 1:5).

2. This approach, it seems to me, emphasizes the primary obligation of the catechist, to be faithful to the message. "Faithfulness" is a central responsibility for the catechist. In our teaching we will want to pass on "the truth, the whole truth, and nothing but the truth." Perhaps the part of that phrase that needs to be emphasized today is "the whole truth." It is not our role as catechists to pick and choose which doctrines, which moral teachings we will share. Some writers have spoken about a tendency to "supermarket Catholicism." This is something we want to avoid. As Avery Dulles has noted, "The Catholic faith is a seamless web made up of the total meaning of all the Christian symbols taken together."[2] Separating out any thread begins an unraveling of the whole beautiful fabric of Catholic faith. A reporter once asked Mother Teresa how she could possibly meet all the needs she encountered. Her reply is meaningful for religious educators: "God does not ask us to be successful — only faithful."

3. Understanding faith as transmission bonds us more closely to the Church. Our mission as catechists is done in the name of the Church and for the Church. It is very interesting again to note that the Apostle Paul himself, that great early catechist, was very concerned that his teaching be perfectly one with Peter and the rest of the Apostles, the first Pope and the bishops. So we read in Galatians:

45

"I went up again to Jerusalem, with Barnabas taking Titus. . . . I laid before them (but privately before those who were of repute) the gospel which I preach among the Gentiles, lest somehow I should be running or had run in vain . . . and when they perceived the grace that was given to me, James and Cephas and John, who were reputed to be pillars gave to me and Barnabas the right hand of fellowship, that we should go to the Gentiles. . ." (RSV Gal 2:1-2, 9-10).

The first letter to Timothy describes the Church as "the pillar and bulwark of truth" (1 Tim 3:15). It is in communion with this Church alone that the truth will be found. It is moreover to the Apostles that Christ gave the first mission to teach, and He gave the Spirit of truth to guarantee that they would guide us in truth. This Spirit remains with their successors who are, according to the Second Vatican Council, the "authentic teachers of the faith."[3] The faithful catechist will want to be in full communion of heart and mind with them.

Catechesis — An Invitation to Faith

Returning now to our suggested definition of catechesis, let us focus on the aspect of "invitation." Even while we faithfully transmit God's love, His plan, His Revelation — we have to remember that faith is above all a gift of God. We can invite people to faith, but we cannot force their acceptance. We have to be patient to let God work in the hearts of those we serve, and He often works slowly. Here the principle enunciated by Paul is very true: one plants, another waters, but God gives the growth (see 1 Cor 3:6).

In inviting, we have to listen and be sensitive to those whom we teach. Our catechetical approach has to be "content-centered," as we have already noted, but it also has to be "person-centered." We should see those whom we teach as being sent to us by God. We should listen to their questions, their fears, their doubts, and never condemn them. If they think we truly care, then they in turn will listen to us. We should pray for our students that their hearts be open to the Spirit. Our catechetical ministry is invitational, not indoctrinational. As Jesus saw some go away and not accept — so, unfortunately, will we.

We transmit the Word of God for the purpose of inviting a response of faith. The Second Vatican Council says that the goal of catechesis is faith, a faith that is "living, explicit, and active."[4] Our efforts are not meant to be passive, languid teachings for laid-back listeners. We have a life-and-death message. We possess a sin-and-grace teaching. We have the solution to sin, suffering, and death and the only secret of happiness that has proven value. We expect a response of faith and have a right to do so.

In this context we do well to be reminded of the words of Pope John Paul II:

> We live in a difficult world in which the anguish of seeing the best creations of man slip away from him and turn against him creates a climate of uncertainty. In this world, catechesis should help Christians to be, for their own joy and the service of all, "light" and "salt." Undoubtedly, this demands that catechesis should strengthen them in their identity and that it should continually separate itself from the surrounding atmosphere of hesitation, uncertainty, and insipidity.[5]

We must, therefore, never share the Good News diffidently or give the impression that it does not matter to us whether or not the listener is changed by the message. Jesus called for faith and praised it when it was expressed. "Whoever would save his life will lose it, and whoever loses his life for my sake will save it. What profit does he show who gains the whole world and destroys himself in the process? If a man is ashamed of me and my doctrine, the Son of Man will be ashamed of him when he comes in his glory" (Lk 9:24-26).

When Peter preached at Pentecost, he wanted a response of faith. Clearly, he had moved his audience by the conviction of his faith and the urgency of his message. "When they heard this, they were deeply shaken. They asked Peter and the other apostles, 'What are we to do?' " (Acts 2:37).

When I say we should look for a response of faith, what do I mean? The topic is catechetically rich, but in its essentials, relatively straightforward. The faith response includes these elements.

1. Faith in the person of Jesus Christ. When Peter and Paul healed a lame man by the Temple gate, they were brought before the Sanhedrin and asked, "By what power or by what name did you do this?" (RSV Acts 4:7). Peter spoke up, "be it know to you all . . . that by the name of Jesus Christ . . . this man is standing before you well [healed]. . . . There is salvation in no one else, for there is no other name under heaven given among men by which we must be saved" (RSV Acts 4:8, 10, 12).

Nothing else should ever distract a catechist from this purpose. The primary focus of faith is the person of Jesus Christ, the total Jesus Christ of the Gospels and Epistles, the real Jesus as proclaimed in every Council of the Church from Nicaea to Vatican II. Those we serve must be helped to believe that in Jesus their deepest hopes for human dignity and fulfillment are really accomplished.

The Second Vatican Council declares: "The Lord is the goal of human history, the focal point of the desires of history and civilization, the center of mankind, the joy of all hearts and the fulfillment of all aspirations."[6] It further affirms, "It is only in the mystery of the Word made flesh that the mystery of man truly becomes clear. . . . Christ . . . fully reveals man to himself and brings to light his most high calling."[7]

48

Only Jesus, the Son of the living God and the son of Mary, can reveal to each man and woman what it means to be human. Only Jesus can let each person know how he or she can find happiness and fulfillment. The more one connects with the person of Jesus in faith, the more that person will become a committed Christian.

2. Faith in the message of Jesus. Jesus was indeed present as a person to the people of His time. His magnetic presence affected them. His love and affection touched them especially in His miracles of compassion. Jesus was a witness to the Kingdom. But Jesus also delivered a message in His parables, His Sermon on the Mount, in wisdom sayings, in His Last Supper discourse, His words from the Cross, and many other words. Jesus was more than a silent witness. He told people what He meant, who He was, and what He expected them to know in order to be saved. In His Bread of Life discourse, He revealed the meaning of the Eucharist. He wanted His message to be accepted in faith. "He who believes has eternal life" (Jn 6:47).

Many of His listeners rejected Him and His message at that point. They did not have faith in His teachings. Jesus then turned to His Apostles and asked them for a response of faith. Peter replied, "Lord, to whom shall we go? You have the words of eternal life. We have come to believe; we are convinced that you are God's holy one" (Jn 6:68-69).

Catechists should solicit a response of faith to the teachings of Jesus, both as found in the Scriptures as well as to the teachings of the Magisterium of the Church as expressed by the Pope and bishops, who are, as the Second Vatican Council says, the "authentic teachers" in the Church.[8]

Jesus did not ask for faith in a culturally acceptable message. He said that what He taught came from His Father. He told His Apostles that they must be accurate reporters of what He taught, so that "He who bears you, hears me" (Lk 10:16). That is what the Magisterium does, under the guidance of the Spirit who abides with the Church as her internal teacher and guarantor of truth. Its teachings apply the message of Jesus to each age and to new issues over the course of the centuries so that the light and power of the Gospel may be ever relevant.

What Is Faith?

Catechists share and witness the person and message of Jesus in order to evoke a faith response in the hearer. What is this faith? A powerful scriptural description of faith is this: "Faith is confident assurance concerning what we hope for, and conviction about things we do not see" (Hebrews 11:1).

Vatican II's Constitution on Divine Revelation says faith is obedience to the call of God. "By faith man freely commits his entire self to God, making 'the full submission of his mind and will to God who reveals,' and willingly assenting to the Revelation given by him."[9]

The very ability to do this is a work of divine grace, an act of the Holy Spirit. The Holy Spirit converts the heart to Jesus. The Holy Spirit makes it easy for the mind to accept and believe Divine Revelation. The Holy Spirit causes maturing in faith so that the understanding of Jesus and His message becomes more profound.

Here is how the Council Fathers expressed it. "Before faith can be exercised, man must have the grace of God to move and assist him; he must have the interior helps of the Holy Spirit, who moves the heart and converts it to God, who opens the eyes of the mind and 'makes it easy for all to accept and believe the truth.' The same Holy Spirit constantly perfects faith by his gifts, so that Revelation may be more and more profoundly understood."[10] Thus the Council Fathers took a resolute stand on the essentially supernatural quality of the faith response. Catechists may plant and water the seed, but God makes the seed come to life and grow.

Finally, Vatican II in the Decree on Bishops, cited above, gives the qualities of faith which catechesis should arouse. It is described as "living, conscious and active."[11] What does this mean?

50

- "Living": not just mental assent but one that changes lives, that leads another person to conversion, to prayer, to friendship with God so that He really matters in their lives.

- "Conscious": a faith that can be expressed and articulated and communicated convincingly to others.

- "Active": faith that leads to action which means that we want to encourage others to be involved in the great moral issues of right to life, social justice, international peace, etc.

Fostering this kind of faith is a big challenge — it doesn't happen in one year. The burden does not rest on any one of us alone. It is the task of the whole Church, but we need to keep our sights set and our goals clear so that our efforts are in full harmony with the teaching ministry which the Spirit is exercising in the Church.

Understanding catechesis as "the transmission of God's Word to invite others to faith" provides a solidly ecclesial framework for this central ministry of the Church. It inserts our efforts into the mainstream of the Church's catechetical mission from the beginning of Church history and enables us to discern how contemporary educational, sociological, theological, or other trends should or should not impact our catechetical efforts.

With this vision of catechesis we are in a position to reflect now on how it can and should respond to some of the major contemporary challenges which are posed by our moment of history.

Discussion Questions

1. How do you understand catechesis as "transmission"? Does this stifle the catechist's creativity?

2. How can the catechist combine the goals of bringing students to both faith in the person of Christ and in His message and teachings?

3. How do you make sure you present the true mystery of Christ — divine and human, and not a watered-down version?

Notes

1. See Thomas A. Groome, *Christian Religious Education* (San Francisco: Harper and Row Publishers, 1980), pp. 20-29.

2. *The Communication of Faith and Its Content* (Washington, D.C.: NCEA Publications, 1987), p. 13.

3. *Lumen Gentium*, Constitution on the Church, no. 25. For the Church's teaching on the role of bishops as "authentic teachers," see this entire section. Read also chapter III on the "Hierarchical Nature of the Church," *Vatican Council II Documents*, edited by Austin Flannery, O.P. (Northport, N.Y.: Costello Publishing Co., 1975).

4. *Christus Dominus*, Decree on Bishops, no. 14.

5. Pope John Paul II, *Catechesis in Our Times* (Boston: St. Paul Editions, 1979), no. 56.

6. *Gaudium et Spes*, Constitution on the Church in the Modern World, no. 5.

7. Ibid., no 22.

8. *Lumen Gentium*, no. 25.

9. *Dei Verbum*, no. 5.

10. Ibid.

11. *Christus Dominus*, no. 14.

Chapter 3

Meeting Today's Challenges

Given the survey of the evolving catechetical context in Chapter One and the reflections offered on the nature of catechesis in Chapter Two, we may now ask: How is the contemporary catechist to respond to contemporary challenges as we move into the Third Millennium of Christianity?

The appropriate response of an effective catechist cannot be to ignore the actual cultural context or to take refuge in techniques or methods that may have been effective in another sociocultural context but are not effective in our setting. The believer relies on the power of the Holy Spirit and looks at the present situation, soberly and courageously, through a process of prayerful discernment.

"Catechesis is not meant to fossilize . . . it needs to be

continually renewed by a certain broadening of its concept, by the revision of its methods, by the search for suitable language and by the utilization of new means of transmitting the message," writes Pope John Paul II. He continues: "The Church cannot but encourage the attempts to create new forms of transmitting the Gospel truth. All the fine initiatives, in this field must be viewed favorably."[1]

The Pope goes on to note that while there must be "adaptation," there are limits, and that Christ Himself has given the example: "He offered his listeners the whole doctrine he had been sent to teach, and in the face of the resistance of those who heard him, he expounded his message with all the demands of faith that it involves . . . he counted on the illuminating action of the Holy Spirit, who would later make understood what he himself was unable to make them understand immediately."[2]

In the light of the Pope's exhortation to catechetical renewal, what principles might contemporary catechists employ as they seek to dynamically and faithfully transmit the Word of God in our culture?

1. Remember the sovereignty of God as the origin and goal of human existence. Our post-religious culture has often attempted to eliminate consciousness of and belief in God. Some formally deny God's existence. Others claim we can say nothing about God. There are people who move beyond the boundaries of their scientific methods and argue that only their intellectual tools can explain the world. And they conclude there is no God.

This leads a current astronomer to say, "The idea that God is an oversized white male with a flowing beard who sits in the sky and tallies the fall of every sparrow is ludicrous. But if by 'God' one means the set of physical laws that govern the universe, then clearly there is such a God. . . . This God is emotionally satisfying . . . it does not make much sense to pray to the law of gravity."[3]

Scientists such as this have a faulty notion of God that

only disowns the product of their own imagination, not the true God of the Bible.[4] Other scientists have a different perspective. "The significance and joy in my science comes in those occasional moments of discovering something new and saying to myself, 'So, that's how God did it.' My goal is to understand a little corner of God's plan."[5]

While individualism and rationalism militate against faith in God and his sovereignty, some people drive the consciousness of God away from their hearts because they do not want their consciences bothered by God's moral demands. The whole of human history has been a story of combat with the forces of evil and will remain so until the last day. The world would make us forget God. That is why Paul demanded, "Do not be conform yourselves to this age" (Rom 12:2). Paul uses the word "world" to mean the vanity and the malice which prevents the "obedience of faith" (Rom 1:5).

The catechist faces, therefore, a twofold phenomenon. First, a culture which has silenced God's presence. Second, a culture which has put autonomous man and woman in place of God. This results in the loss of a sense of being a creature. After all, if there is no creator, there is no creature either. The second outcome is a belief in the untrammeled independence of humans. If there is no higher power to depend on, then what is the point of dependence?

The final result is the most serious — namely, the illusion that happiness is possible without God. Pervasive despair and the loss of hope and confidence are the sad outcome of this foolish belief. The modern obsession with sex, drugs, alcohol, and the acquisition of material goods is a fruitless attempt to find happiness. And it is not working. Happiness can only come by a commitment to the greatest good. The greatest good is God. Those who fail to see this should not be surprised they have reaped a life of unhappiness.

Catechists must do all they can to open their hearers to the reality and sovereignty of God. They should help those they serve to accept this basic truth and focus them on the absolute primacy of God's will as the ultimate norm of all human action. It was Jesus Himself who taught us to say, "Thy will be done." He not only told us to do it, He did it Himself at Gethsemane.

2. Insist on the centrality of Jesus. A catechesis that fails to center on the message of the living Son of God, crucified and risen, will not have an impact. To know Jesus is to know the Father. Catechesis must be Christocentric — Jesus is "the way, and the truth, and the life" (Jn 14:6). This means that catechists must present the person, mystery, and message of Jesus as the chief content of their teaching.[6]

Tragically, studies about biblical literacy tell us that people today do not even know the simplest facts about Jesus, let alone His person. When asked who authored the "Our Father," only 30 percent of the respondents said it was Jesus. A similar low percentage connected Jesus with the Sermon on the Mount. Unfortunately, most people have only a passing acquaintance with the four Gospel portraits of Jesus. Each captures the rich dimensions of the multidimensional mystery of Jesus, and each emphasizes aspects of his teaching that also correspond to other questions and concerns of people today. The superficiality of most Catholics' knowledge about Jesus, "God in man made manifest," is a great sadness and a challenge to the catechist.

Today's catechesis is also often not fostering a passionate personal involvement with Jesus. Paul was so identified with Jesus that he claimed Christ alone was the driving force of his life. "it is no longer I who live, but Christ who lives in me. . ." (RSV Gal 2:20). When Paul wanted to say how significant Jesus was to his hearers, he broke out into a soaring hymn:

> "He is the image of the invisible God,
> the first-born of all creation. . . .
> He is before all things,
> and in him all things hold together. . . .
> For in him all the fullness of God was pleased to dwell,

and through him to reconcile to himself all things,
making peace by the blood of his cross."

— (RSV Col 1:15, 17, 19-20)

That's the music of a man who sees Jesus as the essential
center of every heart and of creation itself. Hence we are called
to tell people both Who Jesus is and what His importance is
for human destiny, dignity, and development. All catechesis
must have a spiritual component in which the hearers are invited to a spiritual union with Jesus. Why else is catechesis
directed to the celebration of the sacraments if not for this
purpose? Every saint, without exception, has testified to the
power of Jesus for their spiritual growth and the presence of
Jesus as the major source of meaning for their lives.

St. Augustine says he would not even be a Christian if
Jesus had not "yelled" at him to get his attention. "You called,
you shouted, and you broke through my deafness. You flashed,
you shone, and you dispelled my blindness. You breathed your
fragrance on me. I drew in breath and now I pant for you. I
have tasted you, now I hunger and thirst for more. You touched
me and now I bum for your peace."[7] The witness of the saints
instructs us on why Jesus should be the center of catechesis.
These vital witnesses of Jesus pry us away from centering our
teachings on someone or something other than Jesus. Our
Church places Jesus before us at every moment, for she is the
Body of Christ in our midst — He lives and acts in and through
this body.

3. Transmit an authentic vision of the Church. The rise
of cultural Catholicism demands of catechists that they counter
this trend with a vision of the real Church. The teachings of
Vatican II are a sure guide in this matter. They especially emphasize three aspects of ecclesiology:

a. The Church is a mystery. This means that the Church
had a divine founder, Jesus Christ, the Son of God. It means
that the cohesive force of the Church is the Holy Spirit. That
means the Spirit holds the Church together whether the social

57

circumstances are favorable or unfavorable. There is no purely human explanation for the emergence, survival, and growth of the infant Church in the face of the world's greatest political opposition, the Roman Empire. In our day, one cannot humanly account for the glorious survival of the Church in Eastern Europe in the face of seventy years of state atheism which used every means of torture, killing, and modern technology's awesome power of propaganda to destroy the Church's faith.

We have plenty of evidence of Christ's prediction that the gates of hell shall not prevail against it (see Mt 16:18). To speak of the Church as mystery is to affirm its divine reality. Yes, God used human processes to bring the Church into existence and continue it. But God used divine power to sustain it.

b. The Church is people. The biblical name for Church is "qahal." It means "called community." Therefore, the Church was not created by the consent of the membership. It came into being because of God's call and intention. Because of the growth in our day of a political understanding of Church, the expression "people of God" has sometimes been reduced to a political meaning. This results in an understanding of Church in which the people of God determine policy and practice by parliamentary procedure.

In the Council texts, "People of God," refers to a community called into existence by God. It is a sacred community that is divine in its origin and destiny. That is why many will also speak of the Church as "communio," because that avoids a politicized description of God's people and returns us to an essentially spiritual meaning of the reality. The Church is a "communio" that reflects the intimate communion of Persons in the Holy Trinity and is the setting in which the redemption of Jesus Christ is experienced.

c. Finally, the Church is an institution. In this intensely personalistic age, it is all too popular to be anti-institutional. The sins of an institution are easy targets. Because the Church is a community of sinners in the process of becoming holy, one need not be surprised that the institution will reflect this.

The Church is therefore a community called to conversion. Instead of pointing the finger at one another, the members need to begin humbly with their own renewal, so that the Church may become all it is called to be.

To say that the Church is an institution reminds us that there are essential hierarchical and juridical elements to its life that are not without the influence of the Holy Spirit. The Second Vatican Council, however, set these elements in the fuller context of the ultimate plan of God for the Church — that it be the means of enabling human beings to share the divine life of the Trinity. All else in the institution is ordered to this sublime end.[8]

There are many other important descriptions of the Church (such as Body of Christ, Sacrament, Herald, and so forth) yet these three aspects can counter reductionist versions of Church which would otherwise make it little more than a transient sociological phenomenon.

4. Emphasize the liturgy, especially the Eucharist. The connection of this point with the foregoing is made eloquently by the Second Vatican Council: "It is through the liturgy, especially, that the faithful are enabled to express in their lives and manifest to others the mystery of Christ and the real nature of the true Church."[9] The transcendent mystery of Christ and the Church is made actual and tangible for people by their participation in the Church's liturgy. Here they encounter the living Christ and are united to him. For this reason the Council teaches that "the liturgy is the summit toward which the activity of the Church is directed; it is also the fount from which all her power flows."[10] The liturgy contains the Church's greatest and most effective catechesis. During the course of the liturgical year, the whole mystery of Christ is relived and the inexhaustible riches of its grace for our lives are assimilated. Set into this cycle, the readings and prayers of the liturgy have a powerful impact on the believer. The catechist will above all want to facilitate the active participation in the Sacred Liturgy of those whom they train and will help them understand the

seasons and rites by which the mystery of Christ is renewed. There is an ancient adage, *"Lex orandi — lex credendi"* (the manner of our worship is the manner of our belief). Nothing will more powerfully strengthen Christian faith and commitment than active and conscious participation with the community in the Church's worship.

At the center of the liturgy, of course, is the Eucharist, Jesus' parting gift of love to his friends and the embodiment of His sacrificial love for them. Scripture scholars agree that the first apostolic preaching was the announcement of the passion, death, and Resurrection of Jesus. The passion narratives were heard at the first celebrations of Eucharist. St. Paul alludes to this when he says, "For as often as you eat this bread and drink the cup, you proclaim the Lord's death until he comes" (RSV 1 Cor 11:26).

In some eucharistic catechesis, it seems that the connection between the Cross and the Eucharist is missing. The fundamental reason for this may well be, as we have suggested earlier, that the link between Jesus and salvation has become too vague. Moreover, people are led to believe that the only purpose for eucharistic celebration is to have community and warm fellowship. An admirable and authentic goal, indeed, but not the whole story.

The clue to a richer understanding of Eucharist is found in the Council documents. "In the most blessed Eucharist is contained the whole spiritual good of the Church, namely, Christ himself, our passover and living bread which gives life . . . through the Holy Spirit. Thus we are led to offer ourselves, our works and all creation with Christ. For this reason, the Eucharist appears as the source and summit of all the preaching of the Gospel."[11]

With no ambiguity, the Fathers teach us the primary divine meaning of the Eucharist and its role as an event of salvation in our lives. We do not gather solely for fellowship reasons. We assemble to experience the salvation of Jesus Christ, won for us by His passion, death, and Resurrection. We come to participate in His sacrificial love so that we may witness that love to each other and to the world.

5. Counter unlimited pluralism with ecclesial pluriformity. There is a certain legitimate pluralism in the expression of God's truth — we have four Gospels instead of one. Each captures different aspects of the one rich mystery of Christ. A truly Catholic (universal) Church will celebrate the mystery of Christ by a pluralism of theologies, liturgical rites, devotional and artistic forms! Yet in the Church's pluralism there is a deep Spirit-fostered unity.

Pluralism, however, is not an absolute value. It is directed to the fullness of truth. It does not justify the attitude that the central questions of life have no final answers. It does not hold that all we can offer are "opinions" and that one opinion is as good as another. While respecting the persons of those who disagree with God's Word, we must not fall into a false tolerance that diminishes the objective value of truth.

Dealing with precisely this issue in the context of Church doctrine, the Extraordinary Synod of Bishops of 1985 in their Final Report note: "It is necessary to distinguish pluriformity from pure pluralism. When pluriformity (a variety of theological, liturgical devotional expressions) is true richness and carries with it fullness, this is true catholicity. The pluralism of fundamentally opposed positions instead leads to dissimulation, destruction, and the loss of identity."[12]

6. Recognize the revealed nature of Christian doctrine. Revelation is the foundation of the Judeo-Christian experience. God takes the initiative to communicate to His creatures truth about Himself and His plan that would otherwise be unknown.

Our faith is not the result of a reflection on human experience but an intervention on the part of God, Who has revealed His saving truth to us: "In times past, God spoke in fragmentary and varied ways to our fathers through the prophets; in this, the final age, he has spoken to us through his Son. . ." (Heb 1:1).

While in a sense all of creation is revelatory of God's goodness and power and while the experience of human life can give us great insight into God's ongoing presence in our lives, catechists need also to be clear that there is a once-for-all delivered "deposit of Revelation" that contains the essential truths about God, His salvation in Christ, and its continuation in the Church. This Revelation was completed by the Apostles and is the normative basis of the Church's teaching for all time. No new revelation is needed. This "deposit of Revelation" contains untold riches of insight and beauty — a rich source of reflection and development for the Church through the centuries — but it can never be contradicted or suppressed.

7. Foster religious literacy. While the goal of catechesis is primarily the fostering of a faith-relationship with God, the relationship has to be expressed and articulated. Catechesis as an instructional activity is very much concerned with this expression, and it must be a primary concern for every serious religious educator.

Religious educators have been perhaps unfairly singled out as solely responsible for religious illiteracy. In fairness, this serious problem must be put in the wider context of American culture and education in general. Recent studies have dealt cogently with this national problem.[13] They document a descent into radical individualism and relativism and a loss of intellectual discipline and vigor on all levels of American education that have left students with only superficial knowledge.

In this context, it is not surprising that surveys of religious education uncover similar weaknesses.[14] *Faith Without Form* is the result of a survey of 784 Catholic high school seniors. The survey showed a hopeful openness to the spiritual in these young people: 95 percent said they prayed — 48 percent as often as daily. They were altruistic in their values, ranking "helping people in need" higher than many self-fulfillment values like high income, having a nice home, car, and other belongings. This and other research validates the experience of many teachers and catechists that young people have a great reservoir of generosity and idealism that is waiting to be tapped.

The troubling part of this book's research, however, is that the authors tell us they find "nothing specifically Catholic or even Christian" in the vague approach to faith reflected in many students. Their concept of God was vague, they reflected little knowledge of Church doctrine or history, and their ideas about morality and sin were very subjective and defined "according to their own desires and convenience."

Given this situation, we shall return in our section on catechetical goals to this important issue. At this point, however, it must be acknowledged that recent decades have seen in some circles in the Church a certain tentativeness about offering the full content of the faith, a glamorization of an approach of questioning, doubt, and searching as if these were values in themselves. The letter to the Hebrews reminds us that "faith is the assurance of things hoped for, the conviction of things not seen" (RSV Heb 11:1).

Catechists today must commit themselves to foster a religious literacy that comes from an assurance and conviction about God's truth. We need to share God's answer to the human mystery, with humility but with confidence.

8. Build bridges between culture and faith. Fidelity to transmitting the Catholic Christian view of life can and must be maintained without sacrificing either relevance or intelligibility. Our mission is to bring the faith to today's real world. This means being sensitive to the modern world's concerns and also seeking to understand critically its thought patterns and language. It must be, however, our humble conviction that we have the values and truth that this modern world is actually seeking.

While the modern world experiences today a clash between a Christian vision of life and one closed to transcendence, Christian catechists proclaim a wisdom to others which recognizes and upholds the priority of ethics over technology, the primacy of the person over things, the superiority of spirit over matter.

Sharing and transmitting these convictions in the modern cultural context has many implications for the methodology of catechesis — a topic to which we shall return later. At this point let us note that one effective way to build the bridge with modern culture is to imitate the methodology of the Risen Christ with the disciples of Emmaus (see Luke chapter 24). He first listens to their concerns and fears with great patience and compassion, and having convinced them of his oneness with them in their situation, He then searches with them the ancient Revelation, the Scriptures, to discover the truth that may cast light on their current questions and experience and lead them to deeper faith in God.

9. Provide living witnesses of faith. The word "witnesses" in Greek comes from the same root word as "martyrs": people who are willing to give their lives for Jesus. In the past the emphasis in catechesis was sometimes exclusively on truths. In today's world people need to know that there are believers whose lives reflect in a real way the relevance of those truths.

Many young people have been taught about faith but have encountered few true living witnesses of that faith. Young people can easily lose faith when they encounter people who teach doctrinal truths but are not living by them, who say one thing and do another. It is this double message that destroys faith and credibility for many.

Parents may take children to church, but when their children hear them talk about money and worldly values all the time or speak hatefully against other peoples or races, the children receive a double message: one cancels out the other.

Modern young people want to see authenticity — living witnesses who integrate faith and life. They do not have to be perfect, but there should not be a discrepancy between faith professed and faith lived. Young people need witnesses like Terry Anderson, held hostage in Teheran under inhuman conditions for more than six years, who emerged saying, "As a

Christian and a Catholic I cannot hate anyone — I forgive my captors!" They need witnesses of service like Dr. Thomas Dooley, Dorothy Day, Mother Teresa, and Jean Vanier. They need witnesses for justice like Archbishop Romero or the American religious women who gave their lives in San Salvador, witnesses for truth like Pope John Paul II.

Paul VI expressed this important point forcefully when he wrote in *Evangelii Nuntiandi*: "Modern man listens more willingly to witnesses than teachers, and if he listens to teachers it is because they are witnesses."[15]

Today's youth also need to find witnesses of faith who live close to them, in their homes, neighborhoods, parishes, schools. They need to see men and women who, despite the pull of materialism and individualism in modern society, live lives of simplicity and of service to others in imitation of the Lord. Such witnesses can help tomorrow's youth discover that they are not powerless against the forces of evil in the world but that through the grace of Jesus Christ they can take their place in the world and in the Church and make a difference.

Discussion Questions

1. What do you think the chief catechetical challenges of our time are? How would you address them?

2. How can you foster a real sense of Church belonging and loyalty among your students?

Notes

1. *L'Osservatore Romano*, January 16, 1985.
2. Ibid.
3. Carl Sagan, quoted in *U.S. News and World Report,* December 23, 1991, p. 61.
4. For a prayerful reflection on this point, see the Book of Sirach, 42:15 through 43:1-35; also Romans 1:18-26.
5. Henry Schaeffer, *U.S. News and World Report,* op. cit. p. 62.

6. See Pope John Paul II, *Catechesis in Our Time*, nos. 5-9, op. cit.; and *General Catechetical Directory* (Washington, D.C.), 1971, no. 40.

7. St. Augustine, *Confessions*, Book 10.

8. *Lumen Gentium*, Constitution on the Church, no. 2. For further reading on this subject, see Avery Dulles, *Models of the Church* (Expanded Edition, New York: Doubleday, 1987) and *The Catholicity of the Church* (New York: Oxford University Press, 1985).

9. *Sacrosanctum Concilium*, Constitution on the Liturgy, no. 2.

10. Ibid., no. 10.

11. *Presbyterorum Ordinis*, Decree on the Ministry and Life of Priests, no. 5.

12. *A Message to the People of God* (Washington, D.C.: USCC Publications, 1986), no. 985.

13. E.D. Hirsch, *Cultural Literacy* (Boston: Houghton, Mifflin, 1987).

14. See also McAuley and Mathieson, *Faith Without Form: Beliefs of Catholic Youth* (Kansas City, Mo.: Sheed & Ward, 1986) and Andrew Thompson, *That They May Know You*, (Washington, D.C.: NCEA Publications, 1982).

15. Pope Paul VI, *Evangelii Nuntiandi*, no. 41.

Part Three
The Goals of Catechesis

Chapter 1

The Catechetical Goals of the Church's Initiation and Socialization Process

In the process of initiation and socialization of its members, the Church expresses its deepest identity. This is why catechesis is so important to the Church. In human terms we could say that the very future of the Church depends on what is happening in the process of initiation, catechesis, and religious education.

While the catechist has a variety of practical concerns that relate to specifics of programming and organization, it is crucial that the catechist have a wider, overarching vision and clear goals. Otherwise, as is said, one can lose sight of the forest for the trees.

I raise this issue because a recent survey of parish directors of religious education revealed some ambiguity and confusion on this subject. Fifty-seven percent of the DREs polled said that it was not clear to them "what knowledge, attitudes, and skills are required to be a Catholic Christian."[1] The author of the article understandably asks: "If the directors of parish programs are unclear about who or what a Catholic Christian is, how can an articulated identity be an intended outcome of their programs?" The same survey, moreover, indicated a consistent ambiguity: 54 percent did not think programs should put more emphasis on Church doctrine, and 62 percent felt no need for the proposed catechism for the Universal Church — a document whose very purpose would be precisely to clarify "what knowledge, attitudes, and skills are required to be a Catholic Christian"!

The lack of a sense of clear goals and intended outcomes among some religious educators is not a result of a lack of official direction and so is somewhat mysterious. The *General Catechetical Directory of the Holy See*,[2] the *National Catechetical Directory*,[3] and *Catechesi Tradendae* of Pope John Paul II[4] all spell out in some detail and with great clarity the goals for catechesis and the intended outcomes which the Church expects from this ministry.

The catechetical goals of the Church's initiation and socialization process are perennial and timeless. They are appropriate goals for A.D. 2000, as they were in decades and centuries past. There will be certain definite new emphases and directions influenced by a reading of the signs of the times, but in a fast-changing world it is good for us also to have a certain sense of ecclesial continuity and stability.

From this point of view I would disagree with those who speak of the Second Vatican Council as causing a radical discontinuity in the life and mission of the Church. To the careful reader of its documents, what is most apparent is the sense of continuity and faithfulness that pervades the texts. There are important new emphases and issues, especially in the Constitution on the Church in the Modern World, but always expressed in the light of bringing the ancient faith to illuminate contemporary questions.

Accordingly, there are certain goals that we are always concerned about in catechesis from the time of the Apostles to the present and into the third Christian millennium. Catechists today need to have the sense of being part of an ancient but living tradition. It is the same Holy Spirit given by the Lord Jesus to the infant Christian community that leads it forward in our day into the future.

Just as we speak of the three R's in secular education, I have found it helpful to summarize the goals of catechesis under five headings — the five C's. These goals are conversion, community, content, contemplation, and commitment. In reflecting on each, we shall reecho some of the themes noted in Part One.

A. Conversion

The consensus of exegetes is that Jesus' core message is one of eschatalogical proclamation — "This is the time of fulfillment. The reign of God is at hand!"— and a call to conversion, "Reform your lives" (Mk 1:15). The message is eschatalogical — referring to the end of time, the eschaton, when God's purposes will reach their ultimate fulfillment. The Good News is the inbreaking of God's love and power (the Kingdom) by means of which "salvation" has finally come with its benefits of forgiveness, healing, and transformation. The "end time" has broken through the march of human history in Jesus' person and mission.

The Church's message and its catechetical expression must radiate this joyful reality. God's initiative, not human effort, has broken through the vicious cycle of human sin and misery and has brought redemption. Truly, "All the ends of the earth have seen / the salvation of God" (Ps 98:3). All the promises and hopes of the Hebrew Scriptures, the Old Testament, have come to realization in Jesus, and our confidence in the ultimate and eternal victory of God's rule is confirmed.

Closely linked to Jesus' joyful proclamation is the call to repentance, to conversion, to holiness. The unconditional love of God does not mean that human behavior doesn't matter. Jesus preached a demanding message of moral reform and conversion, culminating in the exhortation "You must be made perfect as your heavenly Father is perfect" (Mt 5:48). Catechesis must "reecho" this call to conversion, renewal, and holiness.

A message that emphasizes the unconditional love of God in a way that omits or dilutes the call to reform of life is unfaithful to Jesus' most central message. At the earliest grades, catechesis must instill the restless drive for conversion. If it is taught and expressed in small things, it will become an abiding attitude. It is the response to this message that society needs as the solution to its multifold moral and social problems. Tragically, there is not a little truth in the complaint that "It's not true that Christianity has been tried and found wanting; it hasn't been adequately tried."

Fundamental to this attitude of conversion is the conviction noted in Part One about the sovereignty of God, the supremacy of His will, and the acceptance of creatureliness. Jesus, having descended to the human level, gives us the example of this basic level of conversion. From beginning to end, Jesus' whole life was rooted in the attitudes mentioned above. On coming into the world, Jesus said, "I have come to do your will, O God" (Heb 10:7). At the end of His life, His last heart-rending prayer was, "My Father . . . your will be done!" (Mt 26:42).

In an epoch in which personal autonomy and self-assertion are dominant attitudes, the catechist has the opportunity and challenge to communicate a more authentic view of life from a child's earliest age. It is noteworthy how simply children are responsive to this message and how readily they accept their relationship as creatures and children of God. This is a foundation on which we can build a life-attitude of faith-filled submission and conversions.

70

Conversion is a lifelong process. Psychology has emphasized in recent decades the many stages of human moral and emotional development through which people ordinarily pass. Corresponding to these are the ongoing spiritual conversions in which, at each stage of life and in each personal challenge, the believer deepens his or her commitment to God's will and plan. This is the adventure of human living for the believer.

The believer knows that "conversion" is not some kind of rugged self-perfection ego trip in which by willful determination one forces oneself to overcome one spiritual hurdle after another. Rather, it is a prayerful process of surrendering to God's will, letting go of our human, limited defenses, and letting God do His work in our lives. His guidance of our life-journey has been beautifully expressed in God's word to us through the prophet Isaiah: "My burden since your birth, / whom I have carried from your infancy. / Even to your old age I am the same, / even when your hair is gray I will bear you; / It is I who have done this, I who will continue, / and I who will carry you to safety" (Is 46:3-5).

Understanding conversion as the primary goal of catechesis, we perceive more clearly that the knowledge which we attempt to impart in catechetical instruction is intended primarily to undergird and reinforce a personal relationship of discipleship toward the Lord Jesus. Pope John Paul II expresses this goal eloquently:

Catechesis aims, therefore, at developing understanding of the mystery of Christ in the light of God's word, so that the whole of a person's humanity is impregnated by that word. Changed by the working of grace into a new creature, the Christian sets himself to follow Christ and learns more and more within the Church to think like him, to judge like him, to act in conformity with his commandments and to hope as he invites us to.[5]

71

What do the signs of the times tell us in reference to this goal? George Gallup, in the introduction to his 1980 *Religion in America Index*, informs us that his research, polls, and studies demonstrate: "Young people appear to be spiritually restless. They want a strong religious faith, but many at the same time find organized religion today to be spiritually lifeless." The organized church is in many ways the problem for young people. (Yet it can be noted that it is the problem for a lot of adults too.) They perceive the average parish as predominantly concerned with its own temporalities, economies, and survival — rather than the spiritual purpose it exists to serve. This is a complex problem. We simply cannot return to the simple life of the Acts of the Apostles. We can only hope to counteract this obstacle by our emphasis on the life-giving heart of Christianity — the call to conversion to the person of Christ, the challenge to a new way of life based on the Gospel.

In the year 2000, there will be less sociological pressure for people to involve themselves with parish life — it will be more and more widely acceptable to be a non-churchgoer. One will participate only out of conviction. This explains our need to see that this goal of personal conversion to Christ be at the center of our efforts in catechesis today.

This has obvious implications for the new way we present the message. The core of our teaching must be the person of Jesus Christ Himself: "There is no salvation in anyone else, for there is no other name in the whole world given to men by which we are to be saved" (Acts 4:12). Jesus in all His originality and freshness needs to be recaptured and represented. His authenticity will evoke a response in youthful hearts. As one surveys the catechetical documents of the past decade, however, one sees a tension. The documents convey an anxiety that children and young people be systematically and thoroughly presented all the doctrinal and moral elements of the Catholic faith and that they be fully instructed in all the practices of piety and devotion inherited by the Church. This is especially evident in *Basic Teachings* and in Chapter 5 of the *National Catechetical Direc-*

tory. On the other hand, there is an awareness that the person of Christ is the central object of catechesis, that faith growth is developmental and that the capacity of the learner has to be respected (see Chapter 8 of the *National Catechetical Directory* and Chapter 5 of *Catechesi Tradendae*).

It is understandable for those who themselves rejoice in the full personal appropriation of the riches of our Catholic faith to want to see all of this shared, preserved, and passed on. Yet, pastorally it must be admitted many of our young people are not in a developmental stage in which they can find some of our tradition personally meaningful. Perhaps the way out of this dilemma is for Church leaders and catechists to recall the teaching of Vatican II about the hierarchy of truths in *Unitatis Redintegratio*, its Decree on Ecumenism. The *General Catechetical Directory* itself suggests that this doctrinal point has implications for catechesis: "This hierarchy does not mean that some truths pertain to faith itself less than others, but rather that some truths are based on others as of a higher priority and are illumined by them."[6] On all levels, catechesis should take account of this hierarchy of the truths of the faith.

In the light of this principle, it seems to me that in the sociocultural context in which we labor today, in which many of our young people are under-evangelized, our presentation of the message must be strongly Christocentric and oriented to conversion. Being led first to a truly personal faith and conviction about the person of Christ and to a conversion to Him suited to the grace that is given them, they can then be gradually led to a deeper exploration of the fullness of the faith.

One of the first treatises on catechetics, St. Augustine's *Catechetical Instruction* (*De Catechizandis Rudibus*) also took this approach. He noted that since people are moved by the love of another for them, Christ's love should be the center of our teaching: "With this love set before you as an end to which you may refer all that you say, so give all your instructions that he to whom you speak by hearing may believe, and by believing may hope and by hoping may love."[7]

B. Community

From the beginning of Christianity, a community orientation was the first instinct of those who had been converted to Christ by the Apostles preaching. "They devoted themselves to the teaching of the apostles and to the communal life, to the breaking of bread and the prayers. . . . All who believed were together and had all things in common" (Acts 2:42, 44).

Community building must be a major goal of our catechetical efforts as we move toward the year 2000. The Church is the body of Christ, the vine on which we are the branches. We all share the divine life, not only with Christ but with one another. This reality must become a lived experience.

One of the characteristics of contemporary America, many sociologists tell us, is a certain withdrawal, isolation, narcissism, turning in on self. It has been suggested that this may even be the negative side of the renewed emphasis on family. It is a haven, a secure refuge from the pressures and problems of modern life.

Religious individualism is also a characteristic of the American psyche, and a religious privatism is found in many devout Catholics. The experience young people have of parish community is sometimes unfortunate. Sunday Mass appears to be an assembly of isolated individuals rather than a coming together of a caring community. As the sociological supports for faith diminish in our society, there will be a correspondingly greater need for the reality and expression of community to strengthen and reaffirm believers in their lives of faith and witness. It is to this need that Pope John Paul II addresses himself in *Catechesis in Our Time*: "Catechesis runs the risk of becoming barren if no community of faith and Christian life takes the catechumen in as a certain stage of his catechesis. That is why the ecclesial community at all levels has a twofold responsibility with regard to catechesis: It has the responsibility of providing for the training of its members, but it also has

74

the responsibility of welcoming them into an environment where they can live as fully as possible what they have learned."[8]

Reflecting on this goal, the American bishops declared:

As God's plan unfolds in the life of an individual Christian, he grows in awareness that, as a child of God, he does not live in isolation from others. From the moment of Baptism he becomes a member of a new and larger family, the Christian community. Reborn in Baptism, he is joined to others in common faith, hope, and love. This community is based not on force or accident of geographic location or even on deeper ties of ethnic origin, but on the life of the Spirit which unites its members in a unique fellowship so intimate that Paul likens it to a body of which each individual is a part and Jesus Himself is the Head. In this community one person's problem is everyone's problem and one person's victory is everyone's victory. Never before and never since the coming of Jesus Christ has anyone proposed such a community. Community is at the heart of Christian education not simply as a concept to be taught but as a reality to be lived. Through education, men must be moved to build community in all areas of life; they can do this best if they have learned the meaning of community by experiencing it. Formed by this experience, they are better able to build community in their families, their places of work, their neighborhoods, their nation, their world.[9]

Religious educators have a major challenge ahead of them in terms of working at this goal. Two practical observations may be helpful. Community must be "modeled." A parish catechetical staff should see it as a priority, not a luxury, to take time for staff building with CCD teachers or Catholic school personnel. Retreats, days of recollection, faith sharings, common celebration of the Eucharist are essential to help the members to experience their own unity in Christ so that they can plan and work together effectively as community. If this is achieved, they will project something that the children and young people can see and feel, and this will be a great start in educating towards community.

Catholic schools have a special challenge in this area, especially if they are nonparochial. There can be good success in building community in the school setting, but there is little carry-over into the student's parish life. It may even be a subtle means of alienating the student from the parish. It is important to be aware of this and seek ways to overcome it. The young people we teach will be living out their Catholic life as adults in a parish setting and in a parish community. The school should consciously prepare them for this and orient them to this. Perhaps as an initial step, school religion teachers and administrators could initiate meetings with the parish staffs of those parishes from which their students come to find ways of forging mutual bonds and links.

C. Content

Many religious educators recount amusing stories of how small children have massacred religious terms. These episodes bring a needed smile to harried catechists in the midst of their efforts to communicate the faith to little ones, and they provide comic relief for a teachers' meeting.

While we need to avoid overloading small children with technical or theological terms they can't understand, we should be concerned when older children do not recognize some of the more important religious terms which are part of our Catholic heritage. The issue of our students' recognition of religious vocabulary and doctrinal terms cannot be isolated from the broader question of the extent of their intellectual knowledge of the content of the faith itself as it is expressed in the Scripture, the liturgy, and the doctrinal and moral teachings of the Church.

In spring of 1983, the National Commission on Excellence in Education issued a report on public schools in America entitled *A Nation at Risk*. The report said that public school students were showing a decreasing aptitude in the knowledge and skills — especially in areas of mathematics and science — that the nation would need in future citizens if we are to remain competitors with the great industrial societies. John Naisbitt, in his top-ten best-seller *Megatrends*, cites the steep decline in national SAT scores and in other indicators of youths' math and science knowledge. He concludes that today's youths are the first generation in American history to graduate less skilled than their parents!

Some critics of the contemporary catechetical scene might be tempted to write a similar report, entitling it *A Church at Risk*. We know that some of these critics are right-wing ideologues of the Lefebvre school who would reject both the content of Vatican II documents and any implementation of sound psychological principles in catechesis. There are, however, thoughtful critics who ask if our religious education programs as they are currently organized and taught are giving our children and young people the scriptural and doctrinal knowledge, the moral and ethical understandings, the contemplation and service skills that will equip them to live as intelligent, mature, and committed Catholics in the secular and pluralistic society of the Third Millennium.

A National Catholic Educational Association (NCEA) study gives some partial but helpful data with which to examine our programs in the light of some current criticism. The study is contained in the booklet *That They May Know You*. It is based on an analysis of the results of the use by over half a million students in Catholic schools and parish CCD religious education programs of two inventories: one for grade eight (Religious Education Outcomes Inventory — REOI) and one for grade twelve (Religious Education Knowledge, Attitudes, and Practices — REKAP). These inventories question the students' knowledge, attitudes, beliefs, and practices and were designed as a service for the local school or parish to self-evaluate the results of its religion-teaching efforts.

The NCEA study reveals that Catholic students have caught quite well the essential kerygmatic message of Christianity: God's unconditional love for all persons and His personal care of each individual, as well as the redemption and salvation brought by Jesus, God's Son. Catechetical materials affected by the renewal have emphasized these points over the past fifteen years, and the results are grounds for encouragement. The data indicate that the young people's basic perception of the Christian message is positive and hopeful.

Eighty-two percent of the students affirm the unconditional love of God; 79 percent affirm that God made them for a special purpose; 87 percent said they accept Christ as their Savior and Lord; 82 percent affirmed that their faith in Jesus meant a great deal in their lives; 84 percent said that faith in His love made them feel better about themselves; 74 percent knew the Church doctrine that Christ was both divine and human.

There was a very positive correlation found in the study between students' belief about "knowing Christ" and other issues: their conviction that religion answers real questions about life for them; that religious beliefs did make a difference in the way they think and act; their practice of personal prayer.

At this stage in the evolution of American catechesis, it appears that the teaching materials and the efforts of catechists have combined to successfully communicate to those in our school and parish religion programs the central Christian truth of God's love and care for them and the role of Jesus as their Savior.

One specific content area in which students do quite well is that of the sacraments. Since much time is spent on sacramental preparation, especially for First Eucharist and Confirmation, this finding is encouraging. Eighty-one percent of youths in the study said they regularly attend Sunday Mass; 78 percent know the doctrine that the bread and wine are changed into the body and blood of Christ; 68 percent understand that the Eucharist is both a sacrifice and a meal.

Despite these generally positive indications, there are, however, signs that young peoples' actual intellectual knowledge may be shallow and superficial. Clearly their understanding of traditional theological and religious language is poor. The NCEA study indicates considerable room for growth in their knowledge of Scripture, ecclesiology, and traditional Catholic religious terminology.

Only 28 percent could correctly identify the meaning of the basic term "Revelation"; only 27 percent correctly identified the term "Incarnation"; only 25 percent recognized the term "Magisterium"; only 31 percent identified Popes as bishops of Rome; only 37 percent correctly identified the term "infallibility"; only 30 percent recognized the "Immaculate Conception"; while 46 percent knew the meaning of "ecumenism," only 32 percent knew what the "Reformation" was.

Although the vast majority of students readily affirmed that the Bible is the Word of God (87 percent), only six percent of the high school students said they regularly read the Bible, and the answers to specific questions about the knowledge of the Scriptures were very mediocre.

The generous and committed practice of adult Catholic life in the modern world can scarcely be expected to flow from positive and generalized religious feelings alone. While the grace of God is the only ultimate guarantee of a faithful lifelong response to God in the community of the Church, the foundation of firm and well-thought-out convictions about the faith is indispensable. The NCEA study provides more evidence that much more attention needs to be given to this area of catechetical content.

The results of the NCEA study point, I believe, to the need for us as catechists to reflect again on our goals. This in no way means a repudiation of the great gains that have been made in the course of the catechetical renewal of the past twenty years. The clarity and success with which the kerygmatic message is being taught today is an enormous advance on the past. The implementation of sound pedagogical and psychological techniques in our methodology has been a great help.

What we need to avoid, however, is a shallow and superficial presentation of the content of our faith message. We need to be convinced of the importance of solidly and systematically presenting the full scriptural, doctrinal, and historical content of our faith tradition. We need to believe that this is a legitimate and central goal of our catechetical efforts.

We have made much progress in incorporating experiential learning and group activities to make our classes a setting for a "live faith." Have we, however, also imparted a sufficiently thorough intellectual knowledge so that this faith can be intelligent and not dependent on emotional experience or passing enthusiasms?

The earliest catechists, beginning with Paul the Apostle himself, understood their task as transmitting faithfully and clearly the knowledge of facts and teachings that transcended human experience. Scripture scholars point to Paul's repeated use of a precise formula — "I pass on to you what I myself have learned" — in his catechesis on two of the most important dogmas: the Paschal Mystery in 1 Corinthians 15:3-11, and the Eucharist in 1 Corinthians 11:23-28. He sees his task as one to stir up the faith of those he teaches by faithfully transmitting the knowledge and content of mysteries which human reason would never know without Revelation.

The early great theologians of the Church — Irenaeus, Augustine, Ambrose, Cyril — followed the lead of Paul in emphasizing the importance of the accurate and full presentation of the content of the faith as the first and indispensable step in fostering a living and active faith.

At this moment in the catechetical renewal — after having absorbed in our programs many of the methodological advances — it seems desirable to reexamine ourselves on the adequacy of our presentation of the full content of the faith. The Revised Rite of Christian Initiation (RCIA) has made a special rite out of the presentation of the Creed to the catechumen as a high point on the road to membership in the community. By eighth grade, every student in our program should be able clearly and intelligently to explain each of the articles of the Creed to a class and to those who do not share his or her faith. The contents of the Creed should be the object of earnest and systematic study for those preparing for Confirmation.

Beyond the Creed, students in high school should be familiar with Catholic code words, e.g., "Paschal Mystery," "Sacraments of Initiation," "infallibility," "Magisterium," "ecumenism." They should know something of Church history, apologetics, and the Church's social teaching especially on justice and peace issues, which they as citizens must impact with faith-formed values.

One problem for catechesis today is that, with the proliferation of textbooks, there is no uniform expression or definition of even certain key words like "sacrament," "grace," "church." While we wish to defend legitimate pluralism in expression, we may ask if this situation helps the cause of religious literacy or even makes possible conversation or communication between Catholics on their basic religious beliefs.

Participants in an NCEA symposium called to address the results of the NCEA study raised this issue of a common vocabulary for catechetics; and while acknowledging the potential difficulties involved, many felt that something like this should be attempted for inclusion in all catechetical textbooks to promote some kind of unity of faith and expression and to facilitate religious conversation.

A living and active faith is the goal of all catechetical efforts. This involves an appeal to both the head and heart — to the whole person. As we continually reexamine our catechetical approaches and materials, we must be seeking for a proper balance. As this moment that appears to call for a renewed attention to content.

D. Contemplation

Awakening those who participate in our programs to the Transcendent as a lived experience must be a goal of catechesis. While the liturgy is "the source and summit" of Christian life, the quality of our participation in and profit from its celebration is linked to the depth of our prayer life. I will return to the subject again in treating the actual content of catechesis in Part Three.

It may seem pretentious to suggest here that "contemplation" is a goal for catechesis. Why not just say "prayer"? Believe it or not, my reason is more deliberate then just wanting to presume the neat alliterative symmetry of my "five C's"!

Contemplation suggests dimensions to prayer that I believe are broader, richer, and very important in a holistic view of catechesis. First of all, the New Testament message is the story of Jesus' deep personal relationship with "Abba, Father." This is a relationship that is communicated to us by Baptism: "God sent forth his Son born of a woman . . . so that we might receive our status as adopted sons. The proof that you are sons is the fact that God has sent forth into our hearts the spirit of his Son which cries out 'Abba, (Father!)' " (Gal 4:4-6; see also Jn 1:11-12). The Christian life means living out and constantly deepening this relationship, and this requires not just saying "prayers" but serious time given to trustful and loving communion with the Father and the Son. A goal of catechesis has to be to foster this relationship, and that means that there should be a "contemplative" aspect to our approach.

By suggesting a conscious focus on leading our students to "interiority" I am not hoping to foster modern subjectivism in another guise or to suggest another technique for "self-realization." Rather, I believe that we, as catechists, should want to encourage those we serve to practice exterior and interior silence in order to meet Someone: "Here I stand, knocking at the door. If anyone hears me calling and opens the door, I will enter his house and have supper with him, and he with me"

(Rev 3:20). It is to foster this relationship with Father, Son, and Spirit that we need to be concerned about helping others grow in "interiority."

In the context of the year 2000, we will do our students a great service to introduce them to this kind of deeper prayer. They have a right to this intimacy with God as adopted children, brothers and sisters of Christ. Moreover, their earthly lives are likely to be fragmented and harried in our fast-paced modern society. In such a time, silence, solitude, and deep centering on God can introduce an element of sanity and stability into their human lives.

It is tragic that hundreds of young people who were never exposed to the Church's rich heritage of prayer have left us to find an alternative version like Zen and transcendental meditation in Eastern religions.

While our youngsters live in the age of transistor radios and rock music, I believe we can teach them the meaning and the simple techniques of contemplative and centering prayer. This effort would add a whole new dimension to their perception of what the Catholic Christian faith is all about. Too often they are presented with too intellectualized or moralistic a view of their faith that fails to touch the deepest aspirations they are beginning to experience. Serious attention to the contemplative goal of a total catechetical program can help lead them beyond a banal idea of God to a true sense of wonder at the mystery, a Being Who is beyond every effort of our thought, imagining, and feelings. In this way they can discover for themselves the truth of Augustine's famous dictum: "Our hearts are made for Thee, O Lord, and they shall find no rest until they rest in Thee."

Fostering the contemplative dimension of transmitting the Christian faith and experience will evoke the kind of "wonder" and "surprise" that Israel felt in presence of Yahweh and that His hearers felt in the presence of Jesus. This will prevent the faith from being reduced to dry formulae or lifeless practices. It will cultivate the spirit of gratitude and praise.[10]

E. Commitment

Conversion is an all-embracing and abiding goal of catechesis. It should, however, lead to specific expressions. Catechesis must have as a goal to foster commitment to living out the Gospel ideals in the practical circumstances of everyday life. In this context the following points about realizing this goal appear significant to me as we move to the year 2000. I shall also hope to return to this topic in Part Three on the content of catechesis.

1. In terms of personal moral growth, there was much emphasis in the 1970s on the developmental. Workshops applying the principles of Piaget, Kohlberg, and Fowler to catechesis have been offered to countless religious educators. We have all been exposed to the pre-conventional and the post-conventional stages of moral growth. We have been taught valuing techniques à la Sidney Simon and been shown how to help students to "expose" their values and to avoid "imposing" ours in an authoritarian fashion.

All of these insights have undoubtedly helped to some degree our catechetical efforts, and they have been recognized and endorsed in Chapter 8 of the *National Catechetical Directory*. Perhaps this emphasis on the developmental needs to be balanced by a reemphasis on moral principles, on the validity of the objective in moral consideration. Commitment, after all, is to what is objective and ideal. The goal of catechesis is to foster commitment. Personal morality, of course, is a dialectic between the objective and the subjective. The past decade has emphasized the latter; perhaps it is now time to give more attention to the former.

Perhaps this is what Pope John Paul II was calling for in *Catechesi Tradendae* when he wrote: "It is important to reveal frankly the demands — demands that involve self-denial but also joy — made by what the Apostle Paul liked to call 'newness of life,' 'a new creation,' 'being in Christ,' and 'eternal life in Christ Jesus,' which is the same thing as life in the world but lived in accordance with the Beatitudes and called to an extension and transfiguration hereafter." [11]

2. The issue of freedom needs to be more explicitly discussed and analyzed, especially with adolescents. It is natural for them to want to assert their independence and to throw off restraints of adult authorities. This is a necessary part of their growth and the discovery of their autonomy. As every parent knows, a patient and understanding love is required during this period.

This natural desire for freedom is complicated in our moment of history by an ideological promulgation of unrestrained freedom as the highest value. Christian tradition, however, has never seen freedom as absolute. It is always limited by responsibility. The rights of an individual imply duties and responsibilities. Christian freedom is "freedom for" rather than "freedom from." This balance needs to be introduced into our catechesis so that young people may be helped to see that freedom and commitment are not irreconcilable.

3. Catechesis has an even more difficult challenge to teach in our day the concept of obedience. This is a concept that has become almost totally unacceptable to the mentality of modern man, inside and outside the Church. Yet, it is a reality that is at the center of the mystery of our salvation: "He humbled himself, / obediently accepting even death, / death on a cross" (Phil 2:8). Perhaps in this area the catechist may have to assume a prophetic stance in presenting as a value what many may not wish to hear.

4. Moving from the aspects of commitment that focus on its personal expression to its ecclesial and social expression, I would highlight the need for fostering a renewed sense of the call of all to share in the Church's mission of spreading the Good News and of calling all to salvation and faith in Jesus Christ.

The large number of unchurched Americans or indifferent or alienated Catholics should be a challenge to every Catholic. We believe that in our faith we have the greatest treasure.

It is normal to want to share such a treasure, and Jesus has called all to be witnesses. We need to have a missionary attitude, not only to those near us, but toward those uncounted numbers all over the world who do not share the Christian faith.

Pope John Paul II has issued a renewed clarion call to this aspect of Christian commitment in his recent Encyclical letter On the Permanent Validity of the Church's Mission Mandate, His words can help to clarify the goal of commitment for the catechist:

> To us, as to St. Paul, "This grace was given, to preach to the Gentiles the unsearchable riches of Christ" (Eph 3:8). Newness of life in him is the "Good News" for men and women of every age: All are called to it and destined for it. Indeed, all people are searching for it, albeit at times in a confused way, and have a right to know the value of this gift and to approach it freely. The Church, and every individual Christian within her, may not keep hidden or monopolize this newness and richness which has been received from God's bounty in order to be communicated to all mankind.[12]

5. Catechists generally made a very good start in the 1970s toward leading young people to a sense of social morality, to a sense of their duty to do their part for charity, justice, and peace. More effort along these lines will be required in the 1990s.

The signs of the times indicate that excessive national self-interest is going to have to give way to vision that sees us as brothers and sisters of a common humanity sharing a small planet with limited resources. Totally new attitudes will be needed in the American populace as we move toward the turn of the century. Unbridled consumerism will have to give way to a more modest style of life. The instinct to take guns (or bombs) to get the oil we want will have to be tempered by a more wholesome

86

awareness of our mutual interdependence. Commitment to global justice and peace is an important goal for the catechist at this point of history. Fostering this commitment, however, will require teaching wholly new attitudes that may be at variance with much of what the consumer society values.

Commitment to working for respect for life is another aspect that is asked for at our moment of history. Students must be helped to critically evaluate the massive media propaganda which would lead them to undervalue unborn humans or frail and elderly humans.[13]

Discussion Questions

1. Is it realistic to speak of "conversion" as a goal of catechesis? How would the catechist measure or gauge "conversion"?

2. How can the catechetical session "model" Church for students? How can we lead them to committed, lifelong participation in the mission of the Church?

3. What aspects of content do you believe most need to be emphasized today? Why? What aspects of content are most difficult to teach today? Why?

4. What have you found effective in helping lead young people to pray? How can we help them learn the difference between "saying prayers" and praying — being with God in silence, waiting, trust?

5. How do you try to balance current ideas of "freedom" with Christian responsibility? How do you help students rise above a consumerist lifestyle and respond to a call to service?

Notes

1. T. Walters: "Futuring the Present," *The Living Light*, Vol. 24, June 1988.

2. *General Catechetical Directory*, Congregation of the Clergy (Washington, D.C.: USCC Publications Office, 1971).

3. *Sharing the Light of Faith* (Washington, D.C.: USCC Publications Office, 1979).

4. Pope John Paul II, *Catechesi Tradendae*, Catechesis in Our Time (Washington, D.C.: USCC Publications Office, 1979).

5. Ibid., no. 20.

6. *General Catechetical Directory*; op. cit., no. 43.

7. St. Augustine, *The First Catechetical Instruction* (Westchester, Md.: Newman Press, 1962), p. 24.

8. Pope John Paul II, op. cit., no. 24.

9. *To Teach as Jesus Did* (Washington, D.C.: USCC Publications, 1972), nos. 22-23.

10. See Thomas Keating, O.C.S.O., "Catholicity: A Tradition of Contemplation" in *What Makes a School Catholic?* (Washington, D.C.: NCEA Publications, 1992).

11. Pope John Paul II, op. cit., no. 29.

12. Pope John Paul, *Redemptoris Missio*, no. 11. Curriculum material to foster mission awareness in our students is available from the Society for the Propagation of the Faith (366 Fifth Avenue, New York, NY 10001) and the Holy Childhood Association (1720 Massachusetts Avenue, N.W., Washington, D.C. 20036).

13. A helpful resource for conveying the Church's "Respect Life" message is *Choose Life: Unborn Children and the Right to Life* (Washington, D.C.: NCEA Publications, 1991).

Part Four
The Content of Catechesis

Chapter 1

Chief Theological Themes
of Catechesis

The unifying theme of the content of catechesis as presented in the *Catechism of the Catholic Church* is unquestionably the love of God. It's presentation echoes the words of Scripture: "We have come to know and to believe / in the love God has for us" (1 Jn 4:16). This is the real message the catechist brings to the hungry hearts of modern men and women. This is the heart of "the mystery we proclaim."

The *Catechism* expresses this central message of God's saving love by its four pillars. The Creed presents God's loving plan as accomplished in the Son and the Holy Spirit. The sacraments make present here and now God's loving grace for each of us. The Christian Life is our response of love to the love God has shown us — morality is seen as the law of love. Prayer helps to deepen our relationship of love with the Blessed Trinity! This centrality of love in the content of catechesis is underlined by the new *General Directory for Catechesis*: "Jesus proclaims and reveals that God is not a distant, inaccessible Being; a remote power without a name but a Father, who is present among his creatures and whose power is his love" (CCC 102).[1]

The *Catechism of the Catholic Church* presents the content as it was presented in the earliest catechumenate of the Church, focused on what we may call the "four pillars" of catechesis: the Creed, the Sacraments, Christian Life, and Prayer. This ancient Tradition was followed in the Roman Catechism and is again given new vitality in the *Catechism of the Catholic Church*.[2]

It is to be expected that this structure and content would be normative for both the Christian Initiation of Adults (OCIA/RCIA) and for catechetical programs for children and young people. There will be no substitute for a careful reading of the content as presented in the *Catechism*. The following, however, are offered as the author's own reflections on these four sections.

It should be noted that the new *Catechism* reflects a wonderful unity of the content of faith around the theme of "faith": faith professed (the Creed), faith celebrated (the sacraments), faith lived (Christian Life), faith expressed and deepened (Prayer). This unifying theme gives a holistic vision to catechesis and helps avoid a merely cognitive approach.

While we speak of the primacy of the content, it should be understood the "knowing" involved is the kind referred to in Scripture — knowing that involves a total response and surrender to God, not just intellectual assent (see Jn 8:19). Furthermore, this "knowing" requires a morally upright heart and life (cf. Jn 3:19-21). It cannot be acquired by one who has chosen to "live in the darkness."

While the *Catechism of the Catholic Church* deliberately

avoids representing the content of any particular theological school, its heavy reliance on patristic sources justifies seeing in it a fruit of the "nouvelle theologie" which sought to get behind scholastic theology to earlier strata of Christian theological reflection more closely tied to scriptural emphases. There are accordingly four themes that especially characterize the theology of the CCC and that have important catechetical implications for the local catechisms which will come to be developed in its wake: (1) it is clearly revelation-based; (2) it is Trinitarian; (3) it is Christocentric.

The lengthy introductory section to Part One on the creed is a timely exposition of the Church's teaching on Divine Revelation, reminding the reader that there is an "order of knowledge which man cannot possibly arrive at by his own powers" (CCC 50), that gives us the truth about the mystery of God and his plan for the human family. This emphasis on revelation should serve as a corrective to some widespread approaches in contemporary catechesis which seek to make human experience the starting point for the catechetical process. Human experience is an ambiguous reality not unaffected by the sinful condition in which we find ourselves, and it is in no way capable of leading us to the supernatural mysteries that have been revealed. In addition, the excellent treatment on revelation and its transmission (CCC 74-100) should mitigate the ("Protestant") biblicism that has been dominant in some contemporary catechesis, a biblicism that leads to the ignoring of tradition in all of its forms and richness.

The theological orientation of the *Catechism* is strongly Trinitarian and Christocentric and especially emphasizes a favorite patristic theme — the "divinization of man" by incorporation into the divine life. The theological key to reading and understanding the *Catechism* is clearly stated in paragaph 234:

> The mystery of the Most Holy Trinity is the central mystery of Christian faith and life. It is the mystery of God in himself. It is therefore the source of all the

other mysteries of faith, the light that enlightens them. It is the most fundamental and essential teaching in the hierarchy of the truths of faith" [GCD 43]. The whole history of salvation is identical with the history of the way and the means by which the one true God, Father, Son and Holy Spirit, reveals himself to men "and reconciles and unites with himself those who turn away from sin" [GDC 47].

When the *Catechism* subsequently turns in Book Two to the liturgy, it begins with "The Liturgy — Work of the Holy Trinity" (CCC 1077-1112); and when it treats in Book Three of "Christian Living-Morality," it does so in the context of our in-corporation into Christ and our share in his life (CCC 1694-98).

Our introduction to the mystery of the Trinity comes, of course, from Jesus Christ, who reveals God as "Abba" and communicates to us the Holy Spirit. Therefore, the *Catechism*'s Trinitarian focus is necessarily also Christological:

At the heart of catechesis we find, in essence, a Person, the Person of Jesus of Nazareth, the only Son from the Father . . . who suffered and died for us and who now, after rising, is living with us forever" [CT 5]. To catechize is "to reveal in the Person of Christ the whole of God's eternal design reaching fulfillment in that Person. It is to seek to understand the meaning of Christ's actions and words and of the signs worked by him" [CT 5]. Catechesis aims at putting "people . . . in communion . . . with Jesus Christ: only he can lead us to the love of the Father in the Spirit and make us share in the life of the Holy Trinity [CT 5] (CCC 426).

Implicit in the whole project of the *Catechism* and often affirmed in its pages is a theology of faith that again seems to go counter to that reflected in some contemporary theological and catechetical circles. The *Catechism*'s view of faith reflects that of Hebrews 11:1, "Faith is the assurance of things hoped for, the conviction of things not seen" (RSV). It is this assurance and conviction that led the Church to produce the *Catechism*, which it offers not only to the faithful but also to all people as an expression of the Catholic view of the meaning, dignity, and rich promise of human life transformed in Christ. A weary world, confused by a cacophony of competing ideologies, is looking for just such assurance and conviction on the authentic meaning and purpose of existence.

A fourth theme that dominates the context of the *Catechism* is its ecclesial sense. It resists any idea of an individualistic Christianity which is such a temptation in our culture as has been noted earlier.[3]

To those who see the Church only as an institution, the *Catechism* builds on the teaching of the Constitution of the Church of the Second Vatican Council and presents the Church as the universal Sacrament of Salvation (see CCC nos. 774-776). As a Sacrament, the Church has its visible and institutional dimensions but they are of service to Christ and to the Spirit as the means by which redeeming grace is communicated to us. Christ is the only way to salvation and we encounter Him through his sacrament — the visible Church, in her sacraments, teaching, and pastoral structures.

The *Catechism* also presents the Church as Mystery (see nos. 770-775) and as Communion (see nos. 758-759) a newer and richer approach to ecclesiology re-expressed at the Bishop's Synod of 1985 to neutralize the one-dimensional and sometimes political use of the term "People of God." Ultimately, the Church is the place where our communion with the Blessed Trinity is expressed and celebrated.

Discussion Questions

1. What should be the unifying theme of the content of catechesis?

2. What are some of the other major content themes of

the *Catechism* that we need to emphasize in our catechesis?
3. What themes are the easiest to communicate? Why?
What are the most difficult themes to communicate? Why?

Notes

1. An authoritative introduction to the content of the *Catechism* may be found in Joseph Ratzinger and Christoph Schonborn's *Introduction to the Catechism of the Catholic Church* (San Franciso: Ignatius Press, 1994).
2. An exemplary commentary on the content of the *Catechism* is J. DiNoia, G. O'Donnell, R.Cessario, P.J. Cameron, *The Love That Never Ends* (Huntington, Ind: Our Sunday Visitor, Inc., 1996).
3. For an elaboration of this theme, consult F. Kelly, "The Ecclesiology of the *Catechism*," *Josephinum Journal of Theology*, vol. 2, no. 2, 1995.

Chapter 2

The Four Pillars of the
Catechism of the Catholic Church

The Creed: Faith Professed

The ultimate source for the Creed is the actual experience of the history of salvation as lived by the People of God. It is this experience that has given birth to the Creed. Accordingly, the Creed, far from being a dry recitation of formulae, is a prayerful proclamation of the wonderful things God has done and revealed from the Creation through eternal life. It is a revelation of how God has drawn close to humanity to satisfy its longing for Him.

This encounter with God in salvation history evokes from His people the response of faith. This encounter and faith, of course, presume that the human heart is capable and desirous

95

of knowing God. This conviction is fundamental to our profession of the Creed: we believe that to know and love God is the purpose of human life.

Created in God's image and called to know and love God as the fundamental orientation of life, the human person finds many ways to approach God — the material world, the mystery of the human person, etc. But given the situation of fallen, sinful humanity, Revelation is necessary for all people to more easily and securely come to know the true God.

Therefore God, "who dwells in unapproachable light, whom no human being has ever seen or can see" (1 Tim 6:16), has deigned in His great love to reveal Himself and the plan of His love through the history of salvation — from the encounter with Abraham, who thereby becomes the "father of believers," through the sending of His own Son, Jesus Christ, and looking forward to His Second Coming and the eternal Kingdom in which God "will be all in all."

Jesus is, as noted in *Dei Verbum*, the Dogmatic Constitution on Divine Revelation, "the mediator and the fullness of all of Revelation." Hebrews 1:1-2 tells us that "In times past, God spoke in fragmentary and varied ways to our fathers through the prophets; in this, the final age, he has spoken to us through his Son. . . ."

Jesus in turn commanded the Apostles to teach and preach all the saving truths first revealed to them. The apostolic succession of bishops in the Church continues the work of living transmission of the content of Divine Revelation. Scripture and the Church's Tradition embody and express the Revelation, and the Spirit-guided Magisterium of the Pope and bishops keep it alive and relevant and preserve it from distortion.[1]

From the beginning, the Magisterium of the Church has authorized syntheses of this Revelation in the form of "creeds," of which the best known is the Apostles' Creed. It is this Creed which the *Catechism* utilizes to give an expanded and rich meditation on the whole mystery of salvation.

The catechist will want to see to it that participants learn the Creed by memory as a most basic expression of Revelation and that, according to their age and ability, they can explain the meaning of its phrases and the application of each to their lives.

This deeply spiritual exercise of unfolding the Creed should be at the core of catechesis. It may well be that catechetical publishers might wish to rethink their curriculum arrangements and focus major sections of their scope and sequence on the Trinitarian structure of the Creed — Father, Son, and Holy Spirit.

Given the danger of "cultural Catholicism" mentioned in Part One, the catechist will have to make diligent efforts to see that those being taught truly understand the "mystery" the Church professes in the Creed — especially the self-emptying of the Eternal Son in the Incarnation and Crucifixion. The mystery of God-made-man is the center of Catholic faith and the doctrine that truly reveals to human persons their own dignity and worth.

☛ We cannot be satisfied with a catechetical Christology that presents Jesus only as "model" or "brother" — valid as those aspects are in a total Christology. We need to present the mystery of the unity of the divine and human natures of Christ and show how illuminating this is for the deepest desires of human beings. Two of the most outstanding theologians of our day — Hans Urs von Balthasar and Karl Rahner, coming from different approaches — have made this the center of their theology. Somehow, these insights must be captured and "translated" into a catechetical idiom so that we are truly teaching the whole "mystery." The *Catechism* will hopefully be an incentive for this crucial task.

The Sacraments: Faith Celebrated

The sacraments are celebrations of faith, combining the divine action in the here-and-now and the community response and acceptance of God's saving works. In teaching the sacraments today, it seems to me that two basic truths especially need to be remembered and conveyed: (1) The sacraments are direct actions of Jesus Christ for us; and (2) The sacraments are our unique opportunity to respond to Christ.

What is professed in the Creed is not merely the record of past historical events now over and done with. It professes a living and ongoing mystery of God's love. In the awesome words of St. Leo the Great, "Our Redeemer's visible presence [after the Ascension] has passed into the sacraments."[2]

It is for this reason that Pope Pius XII in his Encyclical on the Liturgy, *Mediator Dei*, calls the liturgy "an exercise of the priesthood of Jesus Christ" and therefore superior to all other forms of prayer and devotion.

The challenge for catechists is to help those they serve realize that in the Eucharist and sacraments Christ is now effecting for them all his salvific work in a personal and direct way. In the sacraments they are invited to encounter his "mystery" in the deepest possible way.

A complaint that one often hears from students is that Mass is "boring." While we should do all possible to make its celebration as beautiful and stirring as the mystery it enshrines deserves, the truth is, and we should help students understand, that our participation does not depend on the aesthetic or emotional aspects, but on the deeper reality of what is actually happening when Mass and the sacraments are celebrated.

The current catechetical approach, which focuses on them as "celebrations," needs I believe, to be balanced by a focus on them as "mysteries" in which Christ Himself is present and operative — no matter how unsatisfying the externals may be. At the foundation of the sacraments is the faithfulness of God.

It is this kind of informed faith that has inspired priests and faithful in concentration camps and gulags to find incredible strength and solace in the Mass and sacraments offered with almost no external solemnity to please the senses.

In the Eucharist and sacraments, moreover, the "dialogue of salvation" between God and us is intensified and deepened. The sacraments are our opportunity to respond to God's loving and saving action in and through Christ.

The Mass and sacraments offer us so many ways to affirm our acceptance of God's love and deepen our commitment. The pronouncing of baptismal and confirmation promises, the "amen" to the doxology of Mass and at the reception of Communion, the solemn promises of the sacraments of Holy Orders and Matrimony, the penitent's acts (confession, contrition, satisfaction) in the sacrament of Penance — all are ways and opportunities for us to express and deepen our relationship with God and to respond to His love.

The *Catechism* focuses its treatment of the sacraments on the Paschal Mystery of Jesus' death and Resurrection and on how the mystery is re-presented in the sacraments. It calls on us to make the Paschal Mystery the center of our sacramental catechesis to balance a perhaps too anthropomorphic view of the sacraments as "celebrations of the assembly."

The *Catechism* also evokes the Church's perennial acknowledgement of the central role of the Holy Spirit in its sacramental life — a crucial part of our Trinitarian faith that is often neglected in catechesis. It is the Holy Spirit Who effected the Incarnation of the Son of God and led Him in His Paschal Mystery. It is the Spirit Who brings this mystery to us now in the sacraments and Who sanctifies us through them.

Catechists will want not only to provide a full explanation of the aspects of sacramental theology as described in the *Catechism* but to facilitate the kind of "conscious and active Participation" in them which was called for by the Second Vatican Council. This will mean helping participants understand the rites and symbols involved so that their subsequent participation can be more meaningful.

Christian Life: Faith Lived

The *Catechism of the Catholic Church* should inspire in the catechist a positive and wholesome approach to the teaching of Christian morality. Perhaps no other area of catechesis is in as great a need of strengthening and renewal as is our moral catechesis.

This need also represents a great responsibility for those in charge of the development of catechetical programs. Every sociological survey shows an erosion of adherence to Catholic moral teaching on the part of adults and young people.[3] Many factors can be adduced to explain this distressing trend — the subjectivity of modern culture, the impact of secular media, the worldliness that comes from affluence, and consumerism.

If another contributing cause has been our own neglect, failure, or inadequacy at moral catechesis, then the promulgation of the *Catechism* is a clarion call for a more sustained and serious attention to this area of catechesis. We have to be sure that what we are presenting under the guise of moral catechesis is not some kind of "self-help pop psychology" but the authentic and liberating though demanding ethic of Jesus Christ.

The *Catechism* begins its section on "Life in Christ" with a positive focus on the vocation and dignity of the human person as made in the image and likeness of God and on our call to true happiness. Christian morality seeks to build on these two positive fundamental truths while not neglecting traditional moral codes such as the Commandments.[4]

In this context I have found it helpful in the formation of catechists to focus on five central themes which I believe must undergird and unify our moral catechesis:

1. Moral living is a response to the love of God and the dignity God has given us as sons and daughters: "Live a life worthy of the calling you have received" (Eph 4:1). We do not live moral lives to win God's favor or to force God to let us into eternal life. We do so out of gratitude for the unmerited gifts of God's grace lavished on us through the blood of Christ and the indwelling of the Holy Spirit. Our moral living is to reflect the "new creature" we have become because of God's love.

2. Morality involves lifelong, ongoing "conversion."

Jesus' preaching was capsulized in His proclaiming, "The reign of God is at hand! Reform your lives and believe in the Gospel" (Mk 1:15). Christian morality demands a constant turning away from our inherited sin and darkness. As Paul puts it, we must "put to death" tendencies in us to selfishness, pride, lust, hatred. It is a never-ending struggle, and we need to present this daunting challenge to our students. Christianity is not an "easy street" religion. It is a call to sacrifice, heroism, and generosity. This abstract teaching can be made living by the creative teacher's frequent use of the lives of the saints and Christian heroes who have dramatically embodied this call to conversion.

3. The primacy of God's will is the first step in conscience formation. Society and culture will tell our students that their own needs, feelings, and desires are the primary criteria for action. We are called to teach the countercultural message — that is, that in everything we do, we must seek to discern what God wants. We need to seek God's will manifested in the natural law, in the revealed commandments and teachings of Christ, and in the direction of the Spirit-inspired Church.

4. The reality of sin must be confronted. We must help students acknowledge that to choose deliberately to do what they know to be against God's will is a sin, a rejection of God's love and friendship, and therefore the worst evil that one can commit. This involves communicating the key themes of accountability and responsibility. It is precisely the use of our freedom that sets us apart from the rest of the animal kingdom and gives us our unique dignity. To de-emphasize freedom, responsibility, and accountability is to demean our human dignity. People today seem to speak only of "mistakes" or "bad judgment" — they seek absolution without confession! A powerful catechesis could be developed from 2 Samuel, chapters 11-12, climaxing in David's humble confession: "I have sinned against the LORD" (12:13).

5. The power of grace and the call to holiness must be proclaimed. Despite the power of sin in the world, and even its

influence in ourselves, Paul was able to exclaim: "where sin increased, grace overflowed all the more" (Rom 5:20). All are called to holiness, to ever deeper levels of love of God, self-giving, service to others, and work for the kingdom of truth, justice, and peace.

Christian morality, properly understood and convincingly taught, is a life-enhancing and liberating task. It is our tremendous privilege and challenge as Christian educators to form a generation in the "new life" of Christ.

One precious instrument we have to concretize and celebrate moral catechesis is the sacrament of Penance/Reconciliation. Children and young people imbued with the principles noted above will spontaneously appreciate the value of this sacrament. It is the "place," so much needed in the moral confusion of our day, where confession and absolution go together and where a constant power for ongoing conversion is available.

Prayer: Faith Expressed and Deepened

The decision to create an entire fourth section of the *Catechism* devoted to Christian prayer came late in the process of development of the text and largely as a result of many requests that emerged from the 1990 worldwide consultation on the "pre-definitive" draft of the *Catechism*. The original intent was to imitate the Roman Catechism and include only an appendix with a short meditation on the Lord's Prayer. The decision to expand the treatment on prayer should be seen as a significant intervention of the Spirit speaking through the Church and a response to the thirst of modern people for a deeper relationship with God.

The *Catechism of the Catholic Church* treats Christian prayer under two sections: Prayer in the Christian Life, and The Our Father as the paradigm of Christian prayer. It points out that the faithful believe, celebrate, and live the Christian mystery "through a living and personal, conscious and responsible relationship with God." This relationship is forged, expressed, and deepened by prayer.

There is nothing that catechists can do that is more useful and beneficial in the long term than to help those whom they serve to develop a life of prayer. In this way they bring participants into that "relationship" which alone makes the Christian life possible and fruitful. The testimony of the saints from the beginning is that genuine, frequent personal prayer is indispensable for growth in holiness, growth in the life of Christ within us.

Prayer is traditionally defined as "the raising of the heart and mind to God." This is done with the dispositions taught by Jesus, especially humility, trust, and perseverance (see Mt 7:7-11; Lk 18:9-14; Jn 14:12-13). It is "the humble and contrite heart" that unlocks the gate of divine mercy. Catechists need to point to the example of Jesus, Who Himself retired often to solitude to commune with the Heavenly Father, and to encourage those they serve to find definite times, places, and ways to follow His example.

The *Catechism* cites five distinct forms of prayer — blessing, petition, intercession, thanksgiving, and praise — and it emphasizes the need for incorporating all of these aspects into a regular routine of prayer.

One of the challenges for contemporary catechesis is to overcome a subtle Pelagianism in those we serve.[5] Pelagius was an early heretic who believed that humans by their own power can approach God. The clear scriptural teaching is that we need God's help even for the first approach to God — prayer is itself a gift of God to be sought after and prayed for: "No one can come to me / unless the Father who sent me draws him" (Jn 6:44); "no one can say 'Jesus is Lord,' except in the Holy Spirit" (1 Cor 12:3).

It is to be hoped that the emphasis of the new *Catechism* on prayer will be one of its most special and enduring contributions for the true renewal of the Church and that it will inspire publishers and catechists to make this an even more central part of curricula and programs.

Discussion Questions

1. In what sense is the Creed a "prayer"? How can we help students to see it as the expression of "the mystery we proclaim"?

2. How do you respond to the complaint — "Mass is boring"? How can you develop an appreciation of sacraments in your students?

3. How can we help students see Christian morality not as restricting, but as enhancing happiness and fulfillment?

4. What are some of the different kinds of prayer the *Catechism* encourages? Which ones do we most emphasize? Which ones do we most neglect?

Notes

1. See Vatican II, Constitution on the Church *Lumen Gentium*, Chapter III, especially nos. 24 and 25.

2. Sermon 2 on the Ascension.

3. See, for example, the Gallup Organization Survey of Catholic Attitudes, June 1992.

4. For a good treatment of morality based on the Commandments, see Alfred McBride, *The Ten Commandments: Sounds of Love from Sinai* (Cincinnati, Ohio: St. Anthony Messanger Press, 1990).

5. In one student survey 65 percent of students disagree with the statement that "prayer requires the help of the Holy Spirit" and 22 percent were unsure. See *That They May Know You* (Washington, D.C.: NCEA Publications, 1982).

Part Five
A Methodology for Catechesis

Chapter 1

The Contexts for Methodology

And we speak about them not with words taught by human wisdom, but in words taught by the Spirit, describing spiritual realities in spiritual terms" (1 Cor 2:13).

The criteria for choosing or evaluating a method or an approach for catechesis must be its congruence with the unique ecclesial activity which is catechesis. Catechetical ministry must therefore be rooted in the wider contexts of Divine Revelation and its correlative faith-response, the Ministry of the Word, the evangelizing mission of the Church, and the service of authentic theology.

Catechesis finds its proper place and true meaning only within the ambit of these wider realities, and so the catechist needs to place his or her work in these contexts in order to truly understand and evaluate what are the appropriate and specific catechetical strategies, techniques, and methodologies which are suitable for fostering that "living, conscious, and active faith" which the Second Vatican Council cites as the goal of catechesis.[1]

The catechist therefore will not look primarily to secular pedagogy or social science or psychology for the basis of a method for catechetics. He or she may and should employ helpful insight from these disciplines, but they must always be judged by the criteria drawn from the uniquely ecclesial framework in which catechesis must take place. The goals, the methods, and the teaching strategies of catechetical instruction must correspond to the specific demands of a truly Catholic faith so that those who are served may make "the mystery we proclaim," the full revealed mystery of Jesus Christ, the foundation of their lives. It is with this conviction that I offer these reflections on the ecclesial contexts out of which our catechesis must flow.

Revelation and Faith

Catechesis is based on and directed by Divine Revelation: God's gratuitous intervention in history by which "from the fullness of His love, [he] addresses men as his friends . . . in order to invite and receive them into his own company."[2] God revealed both Himself and the mystery of His will and plan in a process that began with Abraham, climaxed in Jesus Christ, and is continually reflected on by the Spirit-filled Church.

Catechesis serves Revelation by being a means by which its message and mystery are made accessible and relevant to the women and men of each age. The challenge of the catechist is to be faithful to God's word and to help the modern person see how this Revealed Word is the answer to their own deepest longing for truth, goodness, and love. Catechesis therefore is above all at the service of Divine Revelation, and its method must reflect that reality.

Catechesis therefore is at the service of the mystery which

is the subject of Revelation. Wonderful, indeed, is the mystery of our faith, as we say in professing it: "[He] was manifested in the flesh, / vindicated in the spirit; / seen by angels; / proclaimed to the Gentiles, / believed in throughout the world, / taken up in glory" (1 Tim 3:16).

The correlative to Revelation is faith — the grace-inspired response of human beings to God's initiative. Faith is a unique mystery in each individual, and its expression will be influenced by the individual's personal temperament, history, spirituality, etc. Basic to faith, however, is the double acceptance of the Person of God and the content of His message to us.

The past century has seen an evolution in the Church's understanding of Revelation and faith, and consequently in her catechetical methodology. This has been an enrichment for both our theology and our teaching approaches.

The First Vatican Council (1869-1870), in its Dogmatic Constitution on Catholic Faith, placed its principal emphasis on faith as a *sensus intellectualis* — the mind's complete and unqualified acceptance of the truths revealed by God and taught by the Church. The concern was the integrity of truth and the submission of the mind.

The catechetical methodology that flowed from this approach to Revelation was similarly concerned with the correctness of faith-formulas, with propositional truths and statements, and with the intellectual acceptance of the "deposit of Revelation." The Christian faith was presented as a clear and coherent system of truths to be believed, obligations to be fulfilled, and sacramental rites to be observed.

This catechetical approach had and continues to have significant values. It conveyed a respect for objective truth; it gave a clear sense of Catholic identity; it reflected a proper respect for the intellectual aspect of faith. Nonetheless, this approach to Revelation and faith and its catechetical expression were incomplete.

The Second Vatican Council in its Constitution on Divine Revelation (1965) reflected the insights of the intervening century drawn especially from renewed biblical studies and their impact on theology. It recaptured a more dynamic and personalist way of understanding Revelation and faith. It emphasized the finality of Revelation — to create a personal communion of love between God and the human family. It emphasized the historical nature of Revelation as a progressive encounter of God and humans, revealed by words and deeds in the course of salvation history.

In this framework, faith is seen more richly as a total personal response of love to God: "By faith man freely commits his entire self to God, making 'the full submission of his intellect and will to God who reveals' and willingly assenting to the Revelation given by him."[3]

In this view it is clearer that what is revealed is not primarily something but Somebody. There is an interpersonal dynamic, an I-thou relationship, between God and the subject. The Eternal and Invisible God unveils the mystery of His person and manifests it to human persons. The living God enters into a relationship of unexpected intimacy with His creatures. God breaks the silence of eternity, bridges the infinite chasm between Himself and His creatures, and draws close to women and men. This process reaches a glorious fulfillment in the person and mystery of Jesus Christ, Who is in Himself the encounter and union of God and humanity.

This approach to Revelation and faith recaptures the spirit of early Christianity's teaching, reflected, for example in the letter of John: "What we have seen and heard / we proclaim to you / so that you may share life with us. / This fellowship of ours is with the Father / and with his Son, Jesus Christ" (1 Jn 1:3).

Revelation is seen in this view as social and communitarian. It is addressed to and forms a People, a People of God. God "willed to make men holy and save them, not as individuals without any bond or link between them, but rather to make them into a people who might acknowledge Him and serve Him in holiness."[4] Those who respond to God in faith are joined in a spiritual living communion for which Scripture provides many metaphors — the Body of Christ, the Temple of the Spirit, etc.

Revelation is seen as historical. It is not a body of truths dropped prepackaged out of heaven, but it reflects a process of interaction between God and humans and the interplay and interpretation of historical events involving ever greater understanding and penetration as the Spirit leads this People of God forward in its earthly pilgrimage.

This interpersonal encounter with the living God was a shattering experience that seared the depths of the soul. Moses knew he was on holy ground and took off his shoes (see Ex 3:5); Isaiah cried out, "I am a man of unclean lips" (Is 6:5); Peter said to Jesus, "Leave me, Lord. I am a sinful man" (Lk 5:8). The Revelation of the all-holy God always brings with it judgment and a call to conversion.

Revelation and faith, understood in the rich perspective of the teaching of the Second Vatican Council, form the broad framework for catechetical effort and give the basic orientation to catechetical methodology. God's self-gift expects a human self-gift. Revelation calls for a true, personal, unreserved surrender to God. Christianity is not an ideology. It is a Person, Jesus Christ, and "a way" — a way of life based on God's call.

Education in faith must be dominated by these perspectives. It therefore consists primarily, not in imparting a body of religious knowledge for its own sake, but in fostering "knowing" in the biblical sense — a dynamic interpersonal relationship of love between God and persons. The faith-response catechists seek to elicit involves attentiveness and openness to God's presence, Word, and work in people's lives. It involves expectation and listening. It involves acceptance and reciprocity. All this is involved in what we mean by "faith."

Catechesis rooted in this context will seek to facilitate the kind of interior silence and solitude that allow one to open up to the Transcendent God and His love. It will not be dominated by a focus on ourselves, our experience, our present action and human experience, but will seek to transcend human limits "to seek the face of the Living God," to hear His voice and then to apply His Word to our human situation.

A catechetical methodology, influenced by this view of Revelation and faith, will want to help modern people to withdraw from the frenetic pace of modern life, from the tyranny of communications and entertainment media that provide constant but superficial stimulation, and help them to hear the One who says, "Be still and know that I am God" (RSV Ps 46:10 [11]).

Catechesis will accordingly be seen not primarily as an exercise in self-realization but as a opening-up of the mind and spirit to the work of the Holy Spirit. At times this encounter will call our human experience and feelings into the realm of God's judgment. It will always lead to conversion of life and to a countercultural existence.

Revelation and our faith response are then the first and dominant contexts in which to consider catechesis and its appropriate methodology.

This suggests that the catechist should seek to be a channel by which the revealed mystery in all its fullness reaches the ears and the hearts of those being instructed. The catechist, moreover, will seek to be an instrument to help evoke a true personal response of faith in those being served.

The Church's Ministry of the Word

The Church's Ministry of the Word is the second context from which religious education should seek the criteria for developing an authentic catechetical methodology.

Revelation must be made available to each successive generation until the end of time. It is not so much a "deposit" from the past to be preserved, but a "living word" for the present. This is the purpose of the Church's Ministry of the Word. Christ has endowed the Church with the Spirit so that Revelation might be effectively and continuously proclaimed.

Pope John Paul II has recently issued an eloquent and

timely appeal to the Church to recapture its enthusiasm for and commitment to that Ministry of the Word with which it has been entrusted by Christ: "As the second millennium after Christ's coming draws to an end, an overall view of the human race shows that this mission is still only beginning and that we must commit ourselves wholeheartedly to its service."[5] After reviewing historical landmarks in the Church's Ministry of the Word such as the millennium of the conversion of the Slavs and the quincentenary of the evangelization of the Americas, he notes: "Today all Christians, the particular churches and the universal Church, are called to have the same courage that inspired the missionaries of the past and the same readiness to listen to the voice of the Spirit."[6]

The fruit of Revelation, as incarnated in the Scriptures and her Tradition, is the content the Church uses in the Ministry of the Word. The Christ-Event is definitive and normative for all our teaching. This is what is meant when we say "the deposit of faith ended with the last Apostle."

Because Revelation is the context and the norm for the Church's Ministry of the Word, catechists exercising this ministry will seek to base their teaching on Revelation, and therefore their teaching and methods, will, in the words of the *General Catechetical Directory,* be theocentric and Christocentric:

> Christ Jesus, the incarnate Word of God, since he is the supreme reason why God intervenes in the world and manifests himself to men, is the center of the Gospel message within salvation history.
>
> He is "the image of the invisible God, the first-born of all creation. In him everything . . . was created" (RSV Col 1:15). For he stands out as the one mighty mediator through whom God draws near to man and man is led to God (see 1 Tim 2:5). In him the Church has its foundation. In him all things are brought together (see Eph 1:10). For this reason, created things and the con-

science of men and the genuine values which are found in other religions and the diverse signs of the times are all to be thought of, though not univocally, as paths and steps by which it is possible to draw near to God, under the influence of grace and with an ordering to the Church of Christ (see *Lumen Gentium*, 16).

Hence catechesis must necessarily be Christocentric. Just as Christ is the center of the history of salvation, so the mystery of God is the center from which this history takes its origin and to which it is ordered as to its last end. The crucified and risen Christ leads men to the Father by sending the Holy Spirit upon the People of God. For this reason the structure of the whole content of catechesis must be theocentric and Trinitarian: through Christ, to the Father, in the Spirit.

Through Christ: The entire economy of salvation receives its meaning from the incarnate Word. It prepared his coming; it manifests and extends his kingdom on earth from the time of his death and Resurrection up to his second glorious coming, which will complete the work of God. So it is that the mystery of Christ illumines the whole content of catechesis. The diverse elements — biblical, evangelical, ecclesial, human, and even cosmic — which catechetical education must take up and expound are all to be referred to the incarnate Son of God.

To the Father: The supreme purpose of the incarnation of the Word and of the whole economy of salvation consists in this: that all men be led to the Father. Catechesis, therefore, since it must help to an ever-deeper understanding of this plan of love of the heavenly Father, must take care to show that the supreme meaning of human life is this: to acknowledge God and to glorify him by doing his will, as Christ taught us by his words and the example of his life, and thus to come to eternal life.

In the Spirit: The knowledge of the mystery of Christ and the way to the Father are realized in the Holy Spirit. Therefore, catechesis, when expounding the content of the Christian message, must always put in clear light this presence of the Holy Spirit, by which men are continually moved to have communion with God and men and to fulfill their duties. If catechesis lacks these three elements or neglects their close relationship, the Christian message can certainly lose its proper character.[7]

The Ministry of the Word by the catechist in our post-Enlightenment culture will sometimes meet with skepticism and cynicism. This has led to the phenomenon referred to in Part One as "cultural Catholicism" — the approval of persons who wish to retain the name Catholic but who doubt or deny the essential transcendent mysteries on which the faith is built.

There is a great temptation to accommodate to this modern subjectivist culture which sees man's own reason as the ultimate judge and norm of all truth. The catechist has to understand that the life-giving truths which he or she imparts, while not against human reason, are not derived from it but are communicated by God in Revelation and passed on in the Church's Ministry of the Word. The knowledge they bring us of God and of our relationship with Him transcends anything we could imagine or project by unaided human reason. The skepticism and cynicism of the sinful human spirit must be firmly rejected in a joyful act of acceptance of the wonderful "Good News" by a constant act of true supernatural faith.

It is not surprising that recent Popes have dealt frequently with this problem of faith in a secular world. Speaking of the truth of the Incarnation, Pope Paul VI wrote: "Our generation feels the pressure of this great doctrine. . . . Voices repeat with new words, but with old motifs, the wrong answers. He is an extraordinary character, they say; but it is not very clear who he is. It is better to keep on the safe side, and seeming to magnify him morally, they end up by minimizing him essentially. They object to the Catholic doctrine as being mythical, Hellenic, metaphysical, supernatural. . . . The truth counts only to the extent that it is comprehensible; the mystery loses its theological and religious content. . . . We wish to warn you, faithful sons, and with you all those who trust the victorious confession of Peter about this mystery of Christ, the Son of Man — 'You are the Messiah, the Son of the living God' — to remain strong in the faith."[8]

Pope Paul VI warns the modern catechist that our core message is not simply comprehensible to the human mind — the mystery of God transcends the limited abilities of the human mind and must be received and taught as "the mystery of faith." Then it enlarges the human intellect and opens for it new vistas of understanding based on faith and a broader horizon of truth than we might have imagined left to ourselves.

Pope John Paul II adds a deep insight into this same issue by noting that the very nature of the Christian mystery, the kenosis or self-emptying of God, radically challenges and upsets the proud and sinful human intellect. The Holy Father wrote: "To accept the message of Christ, the Divine Redeemer, there is necessary the humility of human reason. Only this humble disposition of mind, which overflows into confidence and adoration, can comprehend and welcome the salvific humility of God."[9]

These truths require that a suitable methodology for catechesis must avoid any temptation at reductionism or silence in the face of the full mystery of Christ in its transcendent totality. On the contrary, catechesis must courageously face the limits which contemporary culture may try to place on its communication of the full truth about Jesus Christ. A proper methodology will seek to make those it serves open to the riches of truth which God alone can reveal, and enthusiastic about the message of life and hope that flows from this revealed truth.

It is in the light of this understanding of the Church's Ministry of the Word that we can appreciate the importance and priority which the Church gives to catechesis — one of the chief expressions of the Church's Ministry of the Word. The Church's code of Canon Law deals with catechetical instruction in Book III,[10] which in fact treats of the teaching office of the Church and the Ministry of the Word. In eight canons the Church highlights the goal of catechesis, "that the faith of the faithful becomes living, explicit, and productive" (Canon 773), and emphasizes the responsibility of pastors and parents to provide opportunities for instruction and formation. It urges pastors to see to the proper training of catechists, especially as regards a proper knowledge of the Church's teaching and the role of good pedagogy (Canon 780).

Evangelization

In his Apostolic Exhortation on Catechesis, Pope John Paul II places catechesis clearly in the ambit of evangelization: "Evangelization — which has the aim of bringing the Good News to the whole of humanity, so that all may live by it — is a rich, complex, and dynamic reality, made up of elements, or one could say moments, that are essential and different from one another, and that must all be kept in view simultaneously. Catechesis is one of these moments."[11]

Evangelization is therefore the wider ecclesial activity which proclaims the Good News of Jesus Christ, crucified and risen, as the Redeemer of humanity. It calls persons to initial faith in Christ and to conversion of life based on the teachings of Jesus. (Pre-evangelization may be a preliminary process that seeks to dispose people to openness to the Good News, to help them see the longing of the human heart for precisely the message proclaimed in evangelization.)

Just as Jesus at the beginning of His mission said that He

came to fulfill the ancient prophecy of Isaiah — "The spirit of the Lord is upon me, therefore he has anointed me. / He has sent me to bring glad tidings to the poor" (Lk 4:18) — so the Church continues His witness, founding her message on the liberating salvation brought by Christ Himself.

Catechesis ideally presumes that there has been a positive response to the work of pre-evangelization and evangelization, and that the person being catechized has in a personal way accepted Jesus' person and message. Therefore catechesis has "the twofold objective of maturing the initial faith and of educating the true disciple of Christ by means of a deeper and more systematic knowledge of the person and the message of our Lord Jesus Christ."[12]

Pastoral practice and experience tell us, however, that often this ideal order of pre-evangelization, evangelization, and catechesis cannot be presumed. The level of faith-commitment of those in our programs may vary greatly, and so dedicated catechists will understand that often they will have to interweave pre-evangelization, evangelization, and catechesis in their presentations.

Pope John Paul shows himself sensitive to this reality when he writes in *Catechesi Tradendae*:

> The specific character of catechesis, as distinct from the initial conversion-bringing proclamation of the Gospel, has the twofold objective of maturing the initial faith and of educating the true disciple of Christ by means of a deeper and more systematic knowledge of the person and the message of our Lord Jesus Christ.
>
> But in catechetical practice, this model order must allow for the fact that the initial evangelization has often not taken place. A certain number of children baptized in infancy come for catechesis in the parish without receiving any other initiation into the faith and still without any explicit attachment to Jesus Christ;

they only have the capacity to believe placed within them by Baptism and the presence of the Holy Spirit; and opposition is quickly created by the prejudices of their non-Christian family background or of the positivist spirit of their education. In addition, there are other children who have not been baptized and whose parents agree only at a later date to religious education: for practical reasons, the catechumenal stage of these children will often be carried out largely in the course of the ordinary catechesis.

Again, many pre-adolescents and adolescents who have been baptized and been given a systematic catechesis and the sacraments still remain hesitant for a long time about committing their whole lives to Jesus Christ, even though they do not actually try to avoid religious instruction in the name of their freedom. Finally, even adults are not safe from temptations to doubt or to abandon their faith, especially as a result of their unbelieving surroundings.

This means that "catechesis" must often concern itself not only with nourishing and teaching the faith, but also with arousing it unceasingly with the help of grace, with opening the heart, with converting, and with preparing total adherence to Jesus Christ on the part of those who are still on the threshold of faith. This concern will in part decide the tone, the language, and the method of catechesis.[13]

The Holy Father's last line is especially noteworthy for the issue of catechetical methodology conceived in the light of evangelization. He says that this concern "will in part decide the tone, the language and the method of catechesis."

Obviously, if we could presume a faith background in those being instructed we could focus all our attention on religious literacy and on the thorough importing of the riches of our Catholic Tradition and heritage. But since this is not the case, the diligent catechist will have to discern how best to foster a yet incipient faith and bring it to that deeper level of understanding and commitment to Christ which would allow the person being catechized to profit from a more systematic and thorough presentation.

This focus on personal faith-development is not a new concern. The need for our methodology to foster personal conversion and commitment was expressed eloquently 1,400 years ago in one of the first treatises ever written on catechesis, cited in an earlier chapter: "With love set before you as an end to which you may refer all that you say, so give all your instructions that he to whom you speak by hearing may believe, and by believing may hope, and by hoping may love."[14]

Our methodology, therefore, must be pastoral and realistic, fully dominated by the concern for evangelization which we have just affirmed. Implicit in this understanding of evangelization and catechesis is a vision of the human person, of God, of the Church, and of Christian life. Doing "evangelizing catechesis" will mean that we must be sensitive in our methodology to this vision.

In this underlying vision behind evangelization, the human person is respected as rational, free, and responsible; God is seen as loving, saving, and inviting; the Church is a Spirit-filled community of believers, and Christian life is a response to God's love, lived in the power of the Holy Spirit.

One might ask if there are teaching methodologies that are distinctively Christian. The answer may be ambiguous. What can be affirmed is that there are teaching methodologies that can be opposed to a Christian vision of the human person, God, the Church, and Christian life. These we must avoid.

Manipulative, coercive, indoctrination-type approaches are opposed to an evangelizing catechesis. They may seem to bring some temporary satisfaction in terms of verbal repetition of formulae, but they can be counterproductive in terms of long-term deeper commitment.

All school children in China learned the sayings of Chairman Mao from their little red books. Their teachers and government were happy, but the experience of Eastern Europe with Marxist ideology has shown how quickly all such indoctrination will be abandoned in the fresh breezes of freedom.

The Christian lifestyle that is the goal of an evangelizing catechesis must be the result of personal conversion as described in Part Two under the goals of catechesis, not the result of efficient brain-washing or coercion. Evangelizing catechesis seeks a growth in personal faith and love that flows from the religious experience of an authentic lived communion with a God truly known and experienced as loving and saving.

Evangelizing catechesis is therefore as difficult and challenging as it is important. It involves the opening of a heart, a spirit, and a mind to the love and truth of God revealed in Jesus Christ and the calling forth of a personal response of commitment. Evangelizing catechesis involves the initiation of believers into a community of disciples who support one another out of deepest conviction and then seek together to witness to the world the values of this Gospel.

This seems to me to be the place to say something about the selection and training of catechists and religion teachers.[15] It is crucial that persons exercising this ministry in the Church possess the underlying vision of the human person, God, and Christian life that we have noted as basic to evangelizing catechesis.

Realistically, in parish programs, it may not always be possible to recruit the "ideal catechist." Often those who respond are not highly educated in biblical or theological sciences, and they are also often distracted by a multitude of other life responsibilities — as parent, spouse, worker, etc.

Granted the many limitations on the pool of available catechists, the evangelization methodology outlined here requires that they have a deep personal faith in Jesus Christ and

119

are willing and able (perhaps with some help from those training them) to express what this faith has meant in their personal lives. They must also be the kind of persons who can accept and love young people as they are, with all their questions and inconsistencies. Finally, they must be persons who love the Church, pilgrim Church though she may be, and respect her shepherds and teachings.

Catechesis and Theology

While catechetics is not theology, there is an interrelation that provides a further context for the methodology of catechesis. Both activities are at the service of the same faith and truth. Both are activities of the Church whose mission is to propagate that faith and truth.

Theology seeks an understanding of the faith in many ways, but essentially it offers its contribution so that the faith may be deepened and communicated. In the authentic Catholic view, it is not an independent intellectual exercise.[16] The primary reality is God's truth — given as a gift to His people, and preserved from error by the Spirit dwelling in the Church and directing the Magisterium of the Popes and bishops. This Magisterium, as the Second Vatican Council again affirmed, is the sole authentic interpreter of the Word of God. Theology is at the service of this truth and should work in close collaboration with this Magisterium.

In his landmark book on theological methodology, Bernard Lonergan highlights the interconnectedness of theology and catechetics.[17] He sees theology "as a set of related and recurrent operations cumulatively advancing towards an ideal goal."[18] These operations he calls the eight "functional specialties" of theology (research, interpretation, history, dialectic, foundations, doctrines, systematics), and he lists the final specialty as communications, under which he includes catechetics.

According to Lonergan, therefore, the total service to the

Word of God should not be exercised without great concern at each stage and by each specialist for the ultimate communication of this truth. A catechetical concern should be present in each theological operation, and Lonergan would appear to reject theories that assert a kind of methodological isolation or independence for any particular branch of theology. Rather, he explicitly insists on the "dynamic unity" of all the disciplines in their service of God's truth.[19]

A legitimate corollary of this assertion, I believe, is the need to reexamine the way in which theology is organized and taught, especially to students preparing for ordained ministry. Sometimes their theology is imparted with little concern for how these students will make its content meaningful and coherent to those to whom they will later preach or teach. It would be desirable that professors of systematic theology work hand in glove with professors of catechetics to see that students are constantly challenged to make the link between the content being studied and the lives and concerns of those to whom they will minister.

In speaking of the eighth specialty, which includes catechetics, Lonergan writes: "It is in this final stage that theological reflection bears fruit. Without the first seven stages, of course, there is no fruit to be home. But without the last the first seven are in vain, for they fail to mature."[20]

Lonergan has a holistic view of the communications-catechetical function which is very helpful in making judgments about religion-teaching methodology and the duties of catechists:

The message announces what Christians are to believe, what they are to become, what they are to do. Its meaning, then, is at once cognitive, constitutive, effective. It is cognitive inasmuch as the message tells us what is to be believed. It is constitutive inasmuch as it crystallizes the hidden inner gift of love into overt Christian fellowship. It is effective inasmuch as it directs Christian service to human society to bring about the kingdom of God. To communicate the Christian message is to lead another to share in one's cognitive, constitutive, effective meaning. Those, then, that would communicate the cognitive meaning of the message first of all must know it.

At their service, then, are the seven previous functional specialties. Next, those that would communicate the constitutive meaning of the Christian message, first of all, must live it. For without living the Christian message one does not possess its constitutive meaning, and one cannot lead another to share what one oneself does not possess. Finally, those that communicate the effective meaning of the Christian message, must practice it. For actions speak louder than words, while preaching what one does not practice recalls sounding brass and tinkling cymbal.[21]

Catechetics and those who produce catechetical texts must take seriously and utilize in their work the results of the preceding seven theological specialties when those results have been examined and endorsed by the institutional instruments through which the Magisterium operates. Thus, it would be irresponsible for a catechist or a publisher to present Scripture in a fundamentalistic way, ignoring, for instance, Pius XII's teachings in the Encyclical *Divino Afflante Spiritu*, the Constitution on Divine Revelation of the Second Vatican Council, or the statements of the Pontifical Biblical Commission. Similarly, doctrinal and moral teaching must be presented in harmony with the best theological insights which have received ecclesial approbation. Conversely, it would be irresponsible for publishers or catechists to propagate the themes of individual theologians or scholars which have not been subject to critical examination and review by other theologians and by the official and authentic Magisterium of the Church. Catechetics is not an exercise in speculative theology but a faithful transmission and fostering of the Church's accepted faith.

In this context, one would endorse the call for catechists and publishers to be sensitive to the principle of the "hierarchy of truths"[22] in presenting the content of catechesis. This relates to the evangelizing concern already mentioned above that impels catechesis to be Trinitarian and Christocentric. It also relates to the theological context of catechesis being developed here. The principle of the "hierarchy of truths" emphasizes for the catechist the organic nature of Christian faith. Certain truths and doctrines are more central and foundational to the rest of the faith than others. The "hierarchy of truths," however, is not to be seen as a "principle of subtraction" whereby some truths can be casually discarded or ignored altogether.

Theology can also helpfully point out to catechists some functions which need to be part of their total concern and also give some help on how they might be carried out.

One Catholic theologian, for example,[23] has pointed to the apologetic, expository, and nurturing functions of catechetics as ingredients that need to be integrated into a holistic catechetical methodology:

a. *Apologetic.* The Church rejects the approach to religion that would base adherence on subjective religious feelings rather than on the historical signs given in the Scriptures, in Jesus Christ, and in the history and teachings of the Church. Therefore the catechist must include treatment of the historical credibility of the faith somewhere in his or her methodology;

b. *Expository.* The Christian symbols of creeds and dogmas need to be presented and explained fully in a meaningful way. The original dogmas of Christianity were contained in the creeds which summarized in a compact form what catechumens needed to know. These creeds and dogmas help to maintain Catholic communion and so must be shared and understood;

c. *Nurturing.* This function relates to the crucial socializing dimension of catechetics, which some specialists have even evolved into an overarching paradigm for catechetics.[24] Realistic catechetical methodology must recognize that the nurturing of the faith is not primarily the task of a classroom alone or of a program but of the whole community of believers. Every effort must be made to help the community understand that it in itself is the chief catechist and all particular efforts at catechesis must consciously relate to the wider community.

One function that is characteristic of theology is the so-called "critical function." Some contemporary writers also urge that the development of "critical thinking" be a more central element in catechetical methodology. It is not always clear what is intended by the exhortation. There is already a "critical" dimension to the basic reality of conversion. This involves a discernment and judgment about where the Gospel of Christ and the values of the world collide. This is a legitimate and desirable kind of critical thinking for catechetics.

The context of these exhortations to "critical thinking," however, sometimes suggest that what is desired by these writers is a critical thinking focused on the Church itself as an institution — her organization, discipline, and practices. It is true that the Church is a pilgrim reality and therefore always in need of renewal because it is composed of sinners. On the practical level, however, it seems unrealistic to be exhorting students who have barely grasped the minimum information and knowledge about their faith to be engaged in a process that requires much more theological background and practical skills at discernment.

At the risk of seeming judgmental, I also feel obliged to point out that many of those making these exhortations are persons who are still heavily involved in religious education as speakers and authors but who themselves have rejected prior ecclesial commitments, as priests or religious. Without making any judgments, I believe one can and should say, in the context of the general thesis of this book, that this situation should not be accepted as a normal or desirable state of affairs. Indeed it can have a subtly corrosive effect on the whole catechetical mission of the Church.

In conclusion, catechists and publishers, striving for an authentic and holistic catechetical methodology, have many elements to bear in mind that come from these four contexts which provide the "ecclesial ecology" in which catechesis takes place. This is not as daunting a task as these reflections might portray. The religious educators who approach their mission with a true "sense of the Church" will instinctively absorb and adopt the values that are suggested by these contexts of catechesis. From these contexts, I believe, one can draw some concrete principles for catechetical methodology which I shall outline in the next chapter.

Notes

1. Second Vatican Council: *Christus Dominus*, Decree on Bishops, no. 14.
2. Second Vatican Council: *Dei Verbum*, Constitution on Divine Revelation, no. 2.
3. Ibid., no. 5.
4. Second Vatican Council, *Lumen Gentium*, Constitution on the Church, no. 9.
5. Encyclical letter *Redemptoris Missio* (Washington, D.C.: USCC Publications, 1991), no. 1.
6. Ibid., no. 30.
7. *General Catechetical Directory*, published by the Congregation of the Clergy (Washington, D.C.: USCC Publications, 1971), nos. 40-41.
8. *L'Osservatore Romano*: Address of December 18, 1968.
9. Ibid.: Address of December 26, 1984.
10. Translation of Canon Law Society of America (Washington, D.C.: Canon Law Society, 1983), pp. 291-293.
11. Apostolic Exhortation *Catechesi Tradendae*: Catechesis in Our Time (Washington, D.C.: USCC Publications, 1979), no. 18.

12. Ibid., no. 19.
13. Ibid.
14. St. Augustine: *De Catechizandis Rudibus* (Ancient Christian Writers Series; Westminster, Md.: Newman Press, 1962), Ch. 4, p. 24.
15. See Alfred McBride, *The Christian Formation of Catholic Educators* (Washington, D.C.: NCEA Publications, 1981).
16. See *Instruction on the Ecclesial Vocation of the Theologian* (Vatican City: Congregation for the Doctrine of the Faith, Libreria Editrice Vaticana, 1990).
17. Bernard Lonergan, *Method in Theology* (New York: Seabury Press, 1979), p. 125.
18. Ibid., p. 125.
19. Ibid., p. 138 ff.
20. Ibid., p. 355.
21. Ibid., p. 362.
22. Vatican Council II: *Unitatis Redintegratio*, Decree on Ecumenism, no. 11.
23. Avery Dulles, *The Communication of Faith and Its Content* (Washington, D.C.: NCEA Publications, 1985).
24. Berard L. Marthaler, "Socialization as a Model for Catechetics" in *Foundations of Religious Education* (New York: Paulist Press, 1978).

Chapter 2

Principles for Catechetical Methodology

The psychological, educational, and sociological sciences have contributed much that might be helpful in the development of a methodology for catechesis, and these have been expounded upon elsewhere by persons with greater competence. In this chapter I intend to present some ecclesial principles for methodology that clearly emerge from a careful reading and comparison of the basic documents of the Church on catechesis, and from the requirements of the contexts that we have just examined.

1. A variety of methods is possible and desirable. "Catechesis is not limited to one methodology," we are told by the *National Catechetical Directory*.[1] Indeed, differing circumstances and settings demand that catechesis should adopt differing methods for the attainment of its specific aim: education in the faith.[2] The social and cultural surroundings in which the Church carries out her mission are many and diverse, and so variety is to be expected. Indeed, Pope John Paul II has said: "The plurality of methods in contemporary catechesis can be a sign of vitality and ingenuity."[3]

The whole issue of indigenization has emerged as a major modern concern. As far back as the first of the great international congresses on catechetics in Eichstätt in 1960, it was asserted that:

> Catechetics adapts itself to the life and thought of peoples, shows due appreciation of their laudable views and customs, and integrates them harmoniously into a Christian way of life. Catechists seek to recognize the special character, manner of thought, outlook, customs and culture of their catechumens. . . . Catechists instruct according to the psychology of the age-group, sex and special circumstances. . . . They seek in patience to correct whatever is false and erroneous but humbly endeavor to mold into the Christian way of life "whatever is true, whatever is honorable, whatever is pure, whatever is lovely, whatever is gracious, if there is any excellence, if there is anything worth of praise, think about these things" (RSV Phil 4:8).[4]

A constant search for ever more effective methods ought to characterize the catechetical effort. This will especially involve utilizing newer communications and learning technologies.

2. Five criteria for evaluating catechetical methods. From the Church documents on catechesis, I would offer five criteria by which the suitability of any method should be judged. I have ordered them in the sequence that seemed to me most important and am content to let the words of the documents about method speak for themselves:

a. *National Catechetical Directory*: It creates "conditions which will encourage people to seek and accept the Christian message and integrate more fully in their living out of the faith."[5]

b. *General Catechetical Directory*: It involves a "differential" approach that varies according to the age, social conditions, and degree of psychological maturity of those who are involved.[6]

c. *Catechesi Tradendae*: It does not mix catechetical instruction on the Christian message and mystery with "ideological views especially political and social ones" — "it goes beyond any kind of temporal, social, or political messianism."[7]

d. It seeks to embody the Christian message and its power in the heart of the local culture, respecting its "particular values and riches," helping "to bring forth from their own living Tradition original expressions of Christian life, celebration, and thought."[8]

e. The language chosen and the method are inspired by the humble concern to stay closer to a content that must remain intact. The method and language used must truly be a means for communicating the whole and not just a part of "the words of eternal life." Thus the choice of method is not to be dictated by "subjective theories or prejudices stamped with a certain ideology" which tends to obscure or corrupt the basic revealed content of catechesis.[9]

3. There are two overarching methodological approaches: inductive and deductive. The inductive method begins from the concrete, sensible, visible world and the tangible experiences of the person being catechized, and then moves towards insights, principles, and conclusions of faith.

The deductive method proceeds in the opposite manner — beginning with general principles in Church teaching and applying them to the situation of the person being catechized.

All methods inevitably employ elements of both induction and deduction, but both the *General Catechetical Direc-*

tory[10] and the *National Catechetical Directory*[11] judge that: "The deductive approach produces its fullest impact when preceded by the inductive."

4. Experiential catechesis can be catechetically helpful. Experiential catechesis can be considered a form of inductive catechesis.[12] Both the *General Catechetical Directory* and the *National Catechetical Directory* note that: "The experiential approach is not easy but it can be of considerable value to catechesis."[13]

The *General Catechetical Directory* expresses it more fully:

> Catechesis should be concerned with making men attentive to their more significant experiences, both personal and social; it also has the duty of placing under the light of the Gospel the questions which arise from those experiences. . . . Experience, considered in itself, must be illumined by the light of revelation. By recalling to mind the action of God who works our salvation, catechesis should help men to explore, interpret, and judge their own experiences.[14]

Jesus Himself utilized an experiential approach. His teaching made ample use of parables that were drawn from real-life situations in nature or in human behavior. From these human examples, He helped His hearers to understand some basic religious truth. Instructively, His examples often involved the use of humor or subtle irony, and He was not above praising the diligence of the wicked in contrast to the tepidity of the devout!

A person's significant experiences, especially those sometimes called "limit experiences" — the birth of a child, vocational commitment, human love, death, separation, loss, etc. — can provide a moment, an occasion of openness, to discover God's love, will, and plan at work in one's life. As such, these experiences can be "teachable moments" to help an individual make personal the objective truths of God's Revelation. In this way "experiential catechesis," properly done, can make the essential link between the truths of faith and the individual's life.

For this to happen, however, there will always be needed the light of the Holy Spirit and the skill of a qualified catechist. Human experience, by itself, need not necessarily lead to a "transcendent awakening" or a deepening in faith. It cannot, by itself, lead to the discovery of such basic Christian mysteries as the Trinity, the Incarnation, the Redemption, etc.

For these important reasons, one must be careful of too glibly stating that the purpose of catechesis is "to discern God in the experience of life." This does a disservice to the basic reality that "the mystery we proclaim" is ultimately beyond the reach of human experience by itself.

Rightly, then, do the documents warn that a proper use of an "experiential approach" is "not without its difficulties."[15] Sometimes catechists who diligently follow the "experiential activities" provided in a teachers' manual are unable to make the essential "faith link" which is the purpose of catechesis. Such activities may consume class time and even be "enjoyable," but if they fail to deepen Christian faith they are not ultimately helpful to catechesis.

Finally, I believe Pope John Paul II in *Catechesi Tradendae* has striven to give a balanced judgment on this issue:

> It is quite useless to campaign for the abandonment of serious and orderly study of the message of Christ in the name of a method concentrating on life experience. No one can arrive at the whole truth on the basis solely of some simple private experience, that is to say, without an adequate explanation of the message of Christ, who is "the way, and the truth, and the life" (Jn 14:6).

131

Nor is any opposition to be set up between a catechesis taking life as its point of departure and a traditional doctrinal and systematic catechesis. Authentic catechesis is always an orderly and systematic initiation into the revelation that God has given of Himself to humanity in Christ Jesus, a revelation stored in the depths of the Church's memory and in Sacred Scripture, and constantly communicated from one generation to the next by a living, active tradition. This revelation is not however isolated from life or artificially juxtaposed to it. It is concerned with the ultimate meaning of life, and it illumines the whole of life with the light of the Gospel, to inspire it or to question it.[16]

5. Formulas and memorization have a role in catechetics. The *General Catechetical Directory* reminds us strongly that "The advantages of the inductive method . . . must in no way lead to a forgetting of the need for and the usefulness of formulas. Formulas permit the thoughts of the mind to be expressed accurately, are appropriate for a correct exposition of the faith, and, when committed to memory, help toward the firm possession of truth. Finally, they make it possible for a uniform way of speaking to be used among the faithful."[17]

As the *General Catechetical Directory* suggests, ecclesial unity does require some incarnation of faith in approved formulas even beyond the Creed. As the Spirit has led the Church to deepen its understanding of the mystery of faith, this content becomes the common patrimony of the Church. For it to be shared, verbal formulas and dogmas are necessary. They foster ecclesial unity in a pluralistic culture and build bonds of community among Catholics of various nations and cultures. This is a tremendous value that deserves to be fostered.

The *Catechism of the Catholic Church* concludes each section with "en bref" formulations of the content contained in each section. It is the hope and expectation of the *Catechism* that these formulations will be utilized in the various national catechisms and programs as the sequels to this *Catechism*.

Finally, Pope John Paul, in *Catechesi Tradendae*, addresses the debate about the role of memorization in catechetics. He writes:

Catechesis has known a long tradition of learning the principal truths by memorizing. We are all aware that this method can present certain disadvantages, not the least of which is that it lends itself to insufficient or at times almost nonexistent assimilation, reducing all knowledge to formulas that are repeated without being properly understood. These disadvantages and the different characteristics of our own civilization have in some places led to the almost complete suppression — according to some, alas, the definitive suppression — of memorization in catechesis. And yet certain very authoritative voices made themselves heard on the occasion of the fourth general assembly of the Synod, calling for the restoration of a judicious balance between reflection and spontaneity, between dialogue and silence, between written work and memory work. Moreover, certain cultures still set great value on memorization.

At a time when, in nonreligious teaching in certain countries, more and more complaints are being made about the unfortunate consequences of disregarding the human faculty of memory, should we not attempt to put this faculty back into use in an intelligent and even an original way in catechesis, all the more since the celebration or "memorial" of the great events of the history of salvation require a precise knowledge of them? A certain memorization of the words of Jesus, of important Bible passages, of the Ten Commandments, of the formulas of profession of the faith, of the liturgical texts, of the essential prayers, of key doctrinal ideas, etc., far from being opposed to the dignity of young Christians, or constituting an obstacle to personal dialogue with the Lord, is a real need.[18]

6. Specific learning objectives need to be articulated.
The Second Vatican Council, as we have noted, states that the goal of catechesis is to foster a faith that is "living, conscious, and active through the light of instruction."[19]

Instruction, however, is a purposeful enterprise and activity. It is a deliberately planned and programmed intervention by which it is hoped to effect a change in the learners' knowledge, beliefs, and behavior. In ecclesial terms this means to foster "faith growth" and "conversion." To actually achieve these goals, planned educational and instructional activities and strategies must be designed and implemented. There must be what one writer, legitimately borrowing from secular educational theory, calls "intended learning objectives":

> The instructional act is composed of four variables — the teacher, the learner, the subject matter, and the learning environment. Effective instruction is the creative interplay of these four variables so that the learners learn. To creatively design this interplay one needs to be clear about the intended learning objectives. Neither the individual teacher nor the community should be involved in the educational process if they have no clear idea of where they want to go. It is no different for those involved in nonschool K-12 religious education programs. Their instructional activities need to have a direction, a goal. This means that clearly stated learning objectives are a must.[20]

Catechetical publishers in the United States have been very creative and helpful in outlining teaching/learning objectives and in developing scope-and-sequence charts for their catechetical series. On the local scene, however, it is crucial that the person responsible for the program helps the catechists to understand and achieve these objectives. This especially seems needed when the catechists are volunteers.

Teachers and catechists at each grade level should know what content and objectives were already covered in the program, which are to be deferred to a later grade, and which are their special responsibility at this time. Fidelity to this principle can give greater focus to each year and avoid the complaint one sometimes hears from students: "We had all that before."

All of these requirements point to the absolute need of having a competent and trained person responsible for the total catechetical program in a school or parish. Effectiveness does not just happen — it is the result of careful planning and execution.

Notes

1. *National Catechetical Directory* (hereafter NCD), no. 176b.
2. *Catechesi Tradendae* (hereafter CT), no. 51.
3. Ibid., no. 55.
4. J. Hofinger and C. Howell, *Teaching All Nations* (New York: Herder and Herder, 1961), pp. 394-400.
5. NCD, no. 176.
6. *General Catechetical Directory* (hereafter GCD), no. 70.
7. CT, no. 52.
8. Ibid., no. 53.
9. Ibid., no. 31.
10. GCD, no. 72.
11. NCD, no. 176c.
12. NCD, no. 176.
13. GCD, no. 74; NCD, no. 176d.
14. GCD, no. 74.
15. GCD, no. 74.
16. CT, no. 22.

17. GCD, no. 73.
18. CT, no. 55.
19. Decree on Bishops, no. 14.
20. Thomas P. Walters, "Where are We Going? A Case for Learning Objectives in Religious Education," *PACE*, no. 18, p. 21 (Huntington, Ind.: Our Sunday Visitor, Inc., 1987-88).

Chapter 3

An Ecclesial Approach
to Catechetical Methodology

Given the context and principles offered in the first two chapters of this part of the book, I would like to offer some practical suggestions for methodology that might be useful for religious educators. I have already noted that there is no one absolute methodology that must be followed and that, whatever approach is taken, will have to make ample adaptation for social, cultural, and developmental factors, utilizing both inductive and deductive approaches.

Nonetheless, the ecclesial approach to catechesis outlined in this entire book represents something of a shift of emphasis from what has been more common in American catechesis, and so I believe it will be helpful to suggest briefly some possible practical strategies that might be considered by those responsible for creating catechetical textual materials and programs. I believe that these suggestions are especially relevant in the light of the need to integrate the orientations of the *Catechism of the Catholic Church* into our programs and materials.

Catechesis in an ecclesial context envisions believers who have already been in some way evangelized and who have made an initial response of faith to the God who has approached them in Jesus Christ. Catechesis seeks in some organized fashion to give growth to this seed of faith, to nourish it, and to develop a deeper understanding of the mystery of Christ and its meaning for the lives of those who are served.[1]

In order for this to happen, I suggest that catechetical methodology might include five steps. These are:

1. Preparation
2. Proclamation
3. Explanation
4. Application
5. Celebration

I shall offer a few thoughts on each step and hope that the creativity of publishers and teachers will give them further development.

First Step: Preparation

This step suggests that the catechist must help create the conditions for the possibility of a deepening of God's Word in the hearts of those being served. This is no easy task in the setting of modern, hectic life in the Western world, where the individual is daily subjected to a barrage of stimuli from the media of communication, advertising, competing ideologies, etc.

Rather than begin catechesis with a focus on one's present experience, which is so inundated with influences that are anything but transcendent, I suggest that the first step needs to be

138

some kind of temporary "calculated disengagement" that helps the believer to become open, docile, and receptive to the absolute truth of God's Word. At a later stage, when the roots of faith have been deepened, the believer will and must turn to reengagement and critical reflection. To focus at the start on the contemporary environment, so riddled with ambiguity and sinfulness, does not seem to me to be the most promising approach for religious education.

Paul the Apostle, it seems, made a brief flirtation with the critical-engagement model of catechesis (see Acts 17:22-33) in Athens but quickly learned that it brought few dividends. Moving to Corinth, he returned to faith in the absolute power of his transcendent message and significantly wrote to the Corinthians: "The natural man does not accept what is taught by the Spirit of God. For him, that is absurdity. He cannot come to know such teaching because it must be appraised in a spiritual way" (1 Cor 2:14).

Accordingly, it seems to me that the first step in catechesis is to devise strategies and approaches that will help participants to be open to the unique wisdom of faith that comes only from the Holy Spirit.

In a practical way, this will mean introducing techniques to foster exterior and interior silence and render participants receptive to the Word of God. Perhaps the goal of this step is reflected in the Gospel image of Mary of Bethany, who "sat beside the Lord at his feet listening to him speak" (Lk 10:39). In this context, I believe we should not see the school classroom physical setting as the desirable one for catechesis. While catechesis has a crucial instructional component, it seeks a total cognitive, affective, and behavioral response. It is desirable, then, that the setting for catechetical sessions have something of the aura of "holy space." A carpeted room, with a cross and Bible properly displayed and with seats arranged in a more communitarian position, would be the preferable arrangement. Such a setting suggests to participants that something important, special, and different will take place here.

Recent decades have seen a rediscovery of the Church's ancient tradition of contemplative and centering prayer. This positive development should be exploited by religious educators to help those they serve to find that "inner room" where they may really commune with the Father and hear His Word. Experience has taught us that even young children will respond positively to a call to contemplative prayer. In this step, inventive catechists will find ways to use appropriate music and other mood-setting devices to help create an atmosphere in which participants can "be still and know that I am God" (RSV Ps 46:10 [11]).

A second aspect of the preparation phase is perhaps even more challenging. The whole post-Enlightenment culture and world-view have so focused Western people on their subjectivity — and consequently on their feelings, desires and will — that the first step of authentic catechesis must be to help people overcome and step out of this self-absorbed environment and into the bright sunlight of the living and loving God.

This first step, therefore, I believe, must be to call believers to acknowledge in depth that "none of us lives as his own master and none of us dies as his own master. For if we live, we live for the Lord, and if we die, we die for the Lord; so then, whether we live or die, we are the Lord's" (Rom 14:7-8).

Overcoming the dominant subjectivity of our culture is a first step and a great challenge for catechesis. It must be done gently, not brusquely, realizing that people are on a complex faith journey in a generally hostile world. Creative catechists need to explore ways of moving in a program from hospitality and true welcome of participants to a true orientation of openness and eagerness for God's Word. As in all the steps suggested here, this "step" may be the work of several sessions, but I believe it is an indispensable prelude to what follows.

Whatever strategies are adopted in this first step must always respect the dignity and freedom of participants and avoid manipulation by the teacher or catechist. Nonetheless, the first step of authentic catechesis needs to be this preparation in

140

which the catechized are called before the living and loving God to hear His Word with an attitude of humble and generous receptivity.

Second Step: Proclamation

The new *Catechism of the Catholic Church* insists in the Prologue that catechesis involves in a central way "transmission" of the content of the faith. Accordingly, it seems to me that, presuming the preparation noted in the first step, the second step of catechesis is the proclamation, the announcing of God's Word. It is this aspect that from the start gave us the word catechesis — coming from the Greek word meaning to reecho, to resound the Word of God.

Primacy in catechetical methodology, therefore, must be given to the faithful and effective announcement of this Word as it is expressed in the Scriptures and in the Church's living Tradition enunciated by its Magisterium and "authentic Teachers" the Pope and bishops — who have the spiritual guidance of the Holy Spirit for their exercise of this task.[2]

This proclamation may interweave deductive and inductive approaches, but the catechist needs to be clear that ultimately the truths being taught are from God, are based on Revelation, and can only make sense with the inner teaching of the Holy Spirit.

"Indeed, the word of God is living and effective, sharper than any two-edged sword, penetrating even between soul and spirit, joints and marrow, and able to discern reflections and thoughts of the heart" (Heb 4:12). The second step of catechesis, which is really the central one, must allow this Word to fulfill its task as described in Hebrews.

The catechist will always be aware that this Word he or she proclaims is simultaneously a "Good News" of God's saving love and a judgment on the sinfulness of humanity. The catechist will be faithful to this double aspect of the Word which he or she proclaims.

To effectively serve this proclamation, catechists must receive proper training so that they have personally understood and assimilated this Word. Serious study of the Scriptures and the Church's doctrinal and moral teaching cannot be neglected if the catechist is to engage in this step of the process competently and effectively. Spiritual formation of the catechist is also an ongoing and absolute requisite for effective proclamation.

One possible danger in this proclamation, not unknown in our day, is that the catechist moves to this step so preoccupied with some personal agenda or issue that the content of catechesis is distorted and is presented through this prism alone. The issue may be legitimate, but if it threatens the integrity of the proclamation, then it is harmful. This can happen in a number of ways — e.g., by a catechist's obsession with a private revelation or personal devotion, or with current issues of "liberation," feminism, etc.

It is this danger which Pope John Paul II is addressing when he notes that "the disciple of Christ has the right to receive 'the Word of faith' not in mutilated, falsified, or diminished form but whole and entire, in all its rigor and vigor. Unfaithfulness on some point to the integrity of the message means a dangerous weakening of catechesis."[3]

The *Catechism of the Catholic Church* now unfolds, in authoritative fashion, the full scope of the proclamation that must be at the heart of catechesis. It will be an excellent measuring rod for all those responsible for catechesis to ensure that a systematic, integrated, and faithful proclamation of the "mystery of faith" is realized.

Third Step: Explanation

From what I have just said it is clear that in my judgment the second step of catechesis involves a respectful and faithful proclamation of the Word of God in which the catechist is scrupulous to be a channel and instrument of something much greater than himself or herself.

In the third step, in a certain sense, the catechists' personal creativity is now more challenged and evoked so that they may help participants come to a deeper personal understanding and assimilation of the message of faith.

The explanation that will be made will, of course, be always in the light of the Church's understanding of the Word, but the catechist is challenged to find appropriate ways to "inculturate" this message so that it can be adapted to diverse groups to whom it is addressed. This will be done by utilizing appropriate pedagogical and andragogical teaching/learning techniques and by tapping into cultural points of reference that can help with the understanding of the message.

Explanation should be done in a participative manner. While the second step as I have outlined it above shows a certain deference to the primacy of God's Word, the third step will seek to "educate" — "to draw out" the meaning of that Word. This will require the active engagement of the participants, so that the relevance of the Word to their life story and to contemporary issues can be brought to light. This will aid in fostering that "maturity in faith" which is a major goal of catechesis.

This third step can make creative use of audiovisual aids, role-playing, personal research, and writing — all adapted to the capacities and abilities of the learners.

This is the step in which participants' doubts and questions need to be honestly addressed. The skillful catechist will know whether this is best done privately or if a group reflection would be helpful. The important thing is for participants to understand that Christian faith is fully reasonable and intelligent, and that, while its object transcends unaided human reason, it does not contradict or demean it but elevates and dignifies it.

This third step is perhaps a good place to urge rediscovery of legitimate "apologetics" as part of the explanation process. If such an exercise was once addressed in too polemical a fashion to fellow Christians, it is still necessary in an age of great pluralism and many conflicting ideologies. A proper explanation in catechesis will always help participants to be able to find "a reason for your hope" (1 Pt 3:15). Our explanation will help present the credibility of the Christian faith and message as well as their special relevance to our times.

The role of memory, as mentioned in the previous chapter, should not be underestimated or neglected in this process. An explanation can very usefully include key sentences and phrases for commitment to memory. This helps deepen the assimilation process and can be a help in providing the words for future conversation on faith topics. The lack of a common religious vocabulary among Catholic students of the past two decades is a significant ecclesial and catechetical problem, which needs to be remedied by including memory exercises in this third step. Catechetical texts should include key words and a glossary of terms to assist the catechist in this task.

Explanation, however, will at its best transcend the merely intellectual and exploit the religious imagination, engaging both right- and left-lobe brain operations.[4] The power of image, story, and symbol to help the Word have its fullest impact on the believer must never be underestimated. Jesus' own example in his rich use of parable and story should be the inspiration for the catechist in designing creative explanations of the Word.

Fourth Step: Application

Knowledge is to enhance life, and in the Christian view religious knowledge is not intended to be sterile but to lead to transformation of the individual and society. However, as Pope John Paul II points out in *Catechesi Tradendae*, "Firm and well-thought-out convictions lead to courageous and upright action."[5] So the step of application of the content of faith presumes, in my judgment, the full implementation of the prior three steps.

In biblical and ecclesial terms, what is hoped for as a result of catechesis is a life of "witness" and "service." In the

144

fourth step of catechesis, as I envision it, the focus is on having the truth and knowledge acquired in the prior steps now bear fruit. This involves a deeper level of conversion in the person being catechized and a commitment to expressing this conversion in his or her lifestyle.

The concept of "witness" is deeply rooted in early Christian experience and writing, always linked to the work of the Holy Spirit in us. Jesus promised His followers: "You will receive power when the holy Spirit comes upon you, and you will be my witnesses in Jerusalem, throughout Judea and Samaria, and to the ends of the earth" (Acts 1:8).

This fourth step of catechesis is intended to facilitate a response to the call to be a witness for the Person of Jesus as the world's only Savior and to His way of life. This is not always easy in a culture in which there has been a great privatization of religion. People are reluctant to give public testimony to their religious beliefs, and yet this is an essential part of the vocation of the baptized person, who shares in Christ's priestly and prophetic mission.

Despite the widespread implementation of the Rite of Christian Initiation of Adults, the overall number of converts to Catholicism has greatly decreased in the United States, while the number of unchurched has greatly increased. Catechists must see it as part of their task to help believers recapture their essential missionary vocation.

The concept of "witness" has renewed relevance in our day, as Pope Paul VI so trenchantly pointed out in his letter on Evangelization: "Modern man listens more willingly to witnesses than to teachers, and if he does listen to teachers, it is because they are witnesses."[6] The catechist must encourage and equip those served to bring to their brothers and sisters the life-transforming Good News of Jesus Christ.

"Service" is the other aspect of this fourth step of application. The Gospel image of Jesus washing the feet of His disciples sets the tone for Christian living: "If I washed your feet — / I who am Teacher and Lord — / then you must wash one another's feet. / What I just did was to give you an example: / as I have done, so you must do" (Jn 13:14-15). The Lord has made just such service the criterion for our ultimate judgment (see Mt 25:31 ff.).

Inculcating "service" in our modern society will be a countercultural challenge. It will mean challenging a consumer society that even creates artificial needs while other human brothers and sisters lack essentials. As the Catholic community moves into upper levels of education, affluence, and influence, this part of catechesis becomes even more demanding.

Much has been written in the past decade about praxis-oriented religious education."[7] This approach has been a beneficial corrective to a too-abstract view of catechetics that did not adequately make the missing link with life and action. My reflections on this step are intended to contribute to this discussion by suggesting that our primary source for this direction might be found less in sociology or political science than in a recapturing of our own deepest scriptural and ecclesial roots. This is the reason that I prefer the scriptural terminology about "witness" and "service."

Fifth Step: Celebration

If the catechetical process begins, as I have suggested, in prayerful attentiveness and openness to the Word of God, I believe that it must also end in prayerful gratitude and praise to God.

The Eucharist is the summit and source of Christian life. It is the celebration "par excellence," but at its core it is thanksgiving — which the Greek word Eucharist means. So we say, "Let us give thanks to the Lord, our God" at the heart of every Mass.

This attitude of thanksgiving and praise is paradigmatic for all of Christian life. We look at the "wonderful things" God has done in the Creation and Redemption and are spontaneously impelled to prayer and praise. This must be a major part and the climax of a catechetical process and methodology that is deeply rooted in the Church's own faith and self-understanding.

Again, creative catechists will find effective ways to execute this fifth step in an inspiring way. The usual three moments of liturgical celebration might give a basic framework: proclamation of the Word, silent reflection, common response. Connected, therefore, to the theme of the particular topic being taught, a Scripture passage might be chosen and proclaimed; a period of silent reflection might follow; and then in common prayer or song, a response might be expressed. Such a framework also becomes an implicit teaching vehicle in itself to demonstrate to participants one way to structure their own prayer life.

The use of symbols can be a powerful strategy in this final step of celebration. In 1992, I was part of a large throng in St. Peter's Square, Rome, for the combined Palm Sunday and World Youth Day Liturgy. After the moving readings and rites of the day, the Holy Father announced the site for the 1992 World Youth Day in Denver, Colorado. As he then stood before the altar, a group of young people from Poland, site of the last Youth Day, came across the square carrying a large wooden cross. From the opposite direction came a group of young people from the United States, and before the Pope the large cross was passed from one group to the other. This very central symbol about the following of Christ, and of the unity of these young people in the one body of Christ, was deeply moving to the whole immense congregation.

The cross should be one of the major symbols we use in catechetical celebrations: "May I never boast except in the cross of our Lord Jesus Christ" (Gal 6:14). Yet, I have noted how rarely catechetical texts suggest its use; there is much utilization of water, flowers, rocks, candles, etc., but great underutilization of the chief countercultural symbol of Christianity — the Cross!

Another opportunity for celebration is to observe the feasts of the saints. Most of the participants in our programs are presumably named after a recognized saint, who is to be a model, encouragement, and intercessor. If the feast of that saint can be connected appropriately to a session, it should be noted and celebrated — perhaps following the structure outlined above: reading of a passage from the saint's writings, silent reflection, and a prayer centered on some symbol appropriate to that saint.

The fifth step, then, should bring together the other four steps and give the session a unity that will facilitate the kind of total response which catechesis should seek — cognitive, affective, and behavioral. It should raise the participants to an expression of loving gratitude to that eternal communion of love into whose embrace they are journeying — Father, Son, and Holy Spirit.

The fact that the *Catechism of the Catholic Church* adds to the traditional catechetical structure of creed, cult, and code a fourth major element — Christian prayer — seems to give support to the importance I would like to give to this fifth step of prayer, contemplation, and celebration in our catechetical methodology.

The *Catechism* emphasizes that the purpose of prayer is to foster a "relationship" with God (no. 2558) — "This is our ultimate goal in catechesis." If we do this well for those we serve, this may well be the most significant long-term effect of our efforts. Such a prayer relationship will open believers up to the power of God's life and love within them and enable them to live a life of true Christian witness and service.

Discussion Questions

1. The GDC (no. 141) speaks of the Church's "incomparable treasure of pedagogy in the faith" mentioning the witness of saints and the personal witness of the catechist and suggesting devotions, prayers, spiritual exercises of different

kinds (e.g., Rosary, Stations of Cross). How do I try to incorporate these various elements of the Church's "treasure of pedagogy in the faith" in my class presentations?

2. How do you understand the difference between the "inductive" and the "deductive" method in catechesis (see GDC 150)? Which approach do you prefer? Why? How would you incorporate each in a sample lesson?

3. To truly be open and receptive to the word of God in the kind of Revelation-based catechesis urged in this Chapter, there needs to be created some "space" in student's hearts and minds; some creative distance and silence from the frantic inundation of external stimuli to which they are constantly exposed. How would you try to create this holy space and distance in structuring a catechetical lesson?

4. The "mystery we proclaim" is supernatural. It reveals truths beyond the power of unaided human reason (e.g., Incarnation, Trinity, Eucharist). How do you deal with the skepticism and hesitation of students immersed in an experiential and scientific culture?

Notes

1. See *Catechesi Tradendae*, nos. 19 and 20.
2. Vatican II, Constitution on the Church, *Lumen Gentium*, no. 25.
3. *Catechesi Tradendae*, no. 30.
4. See Maria Harris, *Teaching and Religious Imagination: An Essay in the Theology of Teaching* (San Francisco: Harper and Row, 1987).
5. Op. cit., no. 22.
6. Pope Paul VI, Apostolic Exhortation *Evangelii Nuntiandi*, no. 41.
7. See the influential book by Thomas H. Groome *Christian Religious Education* (San Francisco: Harper and Row, 1980).

Appendix

Stages of the
Catechetical Movement

The next few pages will illustrate five principal historical stages of the catechetical movement.

The ideal catechetical approach will integrate the values and strengths of each stage to create a holistic and balanced approach to the transmission of the Christian mystery and way of life that will elicit the believer's full cognitive, affective, and behavioral response.

I am indebted to an earlier effort at a schema of these stages done by Carl J. Pfeifer and Janaan Manternach, which I have here substantially modified and expanded.

A. Classical Stage

1565 — The Roman Catechism of the Council of Trent

Influences:	Need to give correct doctrinal responses to Protestant errors
Implicit Theology:	God as the Source of Truth
Implicit Ecclesiology:	The Church guards the Deposit of Faith
Chief Aim:	To accurately communicate the Catholic Faith
Methodology:	• Deductive methodology • Memorization of formulae • Use of question-and-answer catechism
Concept for Catechist:	A teacher of truths
Values/Strengths:	• Respect for objective truth • Respect for the human intellect • Sense of certainty and stability • Fostered Catholic unity • Faith has an answer for ultimate questions
Limitations:	• Engendered a non-historical orthodoxy • Little sense of development of doctrine • Sometimes too artificial a chasm between nature and grace • Relation to human experience often weak and language too abstract

B. Educative Stage

Influences: German educational psychology

Implicit Theology: Same as Classical Stage

Implicit Ecclesiology: Same as Classical Stage

Chief Aim: To help students better to understand and assimilate truths

Methodology: Three steps:
• Presentation
• Explanation
• Application

Concept of Catechist: Teacher assisting in learning of truths

Values/Strengths: • Involved the learners' faculties, senses, imagination, and intellect
• Introduced the idea of a systematic and organized lesson plan

Limitations: Content was better presented but still was often in the rather abstract and theological language of neo-Scholastic theology

C. Kerygmatic Stage
Father Joseph Jungmann (1889-1975)

Influences: Scriptural and liturgical research (culminated in the RCIA)

Implicit Theology: God as Savior-Lover

Implicit Ecclesiology: Church as herald of the Good News

Chief Aim: To call to personal conversion to Jesus Christ and to discipleship

Methodology:
• Focus on God's loving and saving plan (Salvation History)
• Show unity of divine plan from Abraham to the Second Coming of Christ

Concept of Catechist: Witness to Christ's Lordship and mission

Values/Strengths:
• Content becomes more unified around Christ-centered focus
• Unity and direction of God's plan is more evident
• Scripture, liturgy become main sources
• Personal conversion is a major aim

Limitations:
• Past history was so central that God's continuing action was not emphasized
• Link with daily human life and experience was sometimes not adequately made

D. Human Development Stage

Influences: Research from studies in developmental psychology, depth psychology, faith, and moral development

Implicit Theology: God as Mystery

Implicit Ecclesiology: Church as a faith community of responsible persons

Chief Aim: To foster a truly personal response to grace

Methodology:
• Inductive methodology
• Use life and human experience as an opening to faith message
• Develop content tailored to life stages and development

Concept of Catechist: Facilitator of personal response to God

Values/Strengths:
• Awareness of and respect for human growth and development
• More conscious effort to create a link between faith and daily life
• Respect for human values

Limitations:
• Sometimes led to a too anthropocentric approach to catechesis
• Downplayed "revealed" nature of the Christian mystery
• Ignored the wounded and sinful aspects of the human condition
• Could be too narcissistic/individualistic

E. Prophetic Stage
1971 Synod of Bishops — Action for Justice

Influences: Second Vatican Council, Constitution on the Church in the Modern World, liberation movements

Implicit Theology: God as Source of Justice, Peace, Freedom

Implicit Ecclesiology: Church as Servant in the World

Chief Aim: To make participants conscious of their social context and active in changing it in light of the Gospel

Methodology:
• Praxis methodology that encourages learners to reflect on current experience and ways to change society
• Utilizes "pedagogy of the oppressed"

Concept of Catechist: Partner in transformation of society

Values/Strengths:
• Recognition of Gospel as leaven in society and of Church as "light to the nations"
• Overcomes dichotomy between faith and life
• Highlights involvement and commitment
• Calls Catholics to remedy both symptoms and causes of injustice

Limitations:
• Can lead to neglect of prayer and contemplation, forgetful of "mystery"

Limitations (continued):

- Danger of overfixation on this life and this earth as ultimate realities
- Political movements come to be seen as "messianic"

Our Sunday Visitor...
Your Source for Discovering the Riches of the Catholic Faith

Our Sunday Visitor has an extensive line of materials for young children, teens, and adults. Our books, Bibles, booklets, CD-ROMs, audios, and videos are available in bookstores worldwide.

To receive a FREE full-line catalog or for more information, call **Our Sunday Visitor** at **1-800-348-2440**. Or write, **Our Sunday Visitor /** 200 Noll Plaza / Huntington, IN 46750.

Please send me: __ A catalog
Please send me materials on:
  __ Apologetics and catechetics   __ Reference works
  __ Prayer books   __ Heritage and the saints
  __ The family   __ The parish

Name_____

Address_____Apt._____

City_____State ____Zip_____

Telephone (   ) _____

                                                        A93BBABP

Please send a friend: __ A catalog
Please send a friend materials on:
  __ Apologetics and catechetics   __ Reference works
  __ Prayer books   __ Heritage and the saints
  __ The family   __ The parish

Name_____

Address_____Apt._____

City_____State ____Zip_____

Telephone (   ) _____

                                                        A93BBABP

Our Sunday Visitor
200 Noll Plaza
Huntington, IN 46750
1-800-348-2440
osvbooks@osv.com

Your Source for Discovering the Riches of the Catholic Faith